D1443821

Discovering Thessalonians

THE GUIDEPOSTS HOME BIBLE STUDY PROGRAM

Floyd W. Thatcher   *General Editor*
Robin White Goode   *Associate Editor*
Bob E. Patterson   *Technical Consultant*

EDITORIAL ADVISORY BOARD

Lloyd J. Ogilvie
Senior Minister, First Presbyterian Church of Hollywood

David A. Hubbard
President, Fuller Theological Seminary

Charles L. Allen
Senior Minister Emeritus, First United Methodist Church of Houston

Ruth Stafford Peale
President, Foundation for Christian Living; Vice President, American Bible Society

Myron S. Augsburger
Pastor, Washington Community Fellowship Church—Mennonite Church

David L. McKenna
President, Asbury Theological Seminary

Russell H. Dilday, Jr.
President, Southwestern Baptist Theological Seminary

The Epistle of Paul the Apostle to the THESSALONIANS

Discovering Thessalonians	Gerald Borchert
What This Scripture Means to Me	Carolyn Huffman
Photographs	Bruce C. Cresson
Book Design	Elizabeth Woll
Cover Artist	Ben Wolhberg

DISCOVERING THESSALONIANS

The Guideposts Home Bible Study Program

GUIDEPOSTS

Carmel   New York   10512

THE GUIDEPOSTS HOME BIBLE STUDY PROGRAM
The Epistle of Paul the Apostle to the Thessalonians:
    1. DISCOVERING THESSALONIANS
    2. My Working Bible
    3. Knowing More About Thessalonians

COPYRIGHT © 1986 by GUIDEPOSTS ASSOCIATES, INC.
      Carmel, N.Y. 10512

All rights reserved. No part of this program or publications within this program
may be reproduced, stored in a retrieval system, or transmitted in any form by
any means, electronic, mechanical, photocopying, recording or otherwise,
without the written permission of the publisher, Guideposts Associates, Inc.,
Carmel, New York 10512.

All Scripture verses referenced herein are from the King James Version of the
Bible.

Designed by Elizabeth Woll.

Printed in the United States of America.

Contents

How to Use
the Guideposts Home
Bible Study Program

1. Read the passages in your *Working Bible* that are included in the appropriate lesson material in *Discovering Thessalonians*. In the margins of your *Working Bible* jot down any notes you'd like to call special attention to.
2. Then, to amplify the Scriptures you've read, study Lesson 1 in *Discovering Thessalonians*. As you read the lesson keep your *Working Bible* open so you can look up the many Scripture references that are included in the lesson.
3. When you complete each lesson, quiz yourself on what you've learned, with the quiz booklet, *Knowing More About Thessalonians*.

Repeat this rhythm as you read each lesson, to get the most from your study of God's Word.

Publisher's Introduction

As we come now to our studies of 1 and 2 Thessalonians, it will be helpful to remember that we are reading the very first of Paul's writings. It will also be helpful for us to remember that these early Christians to whom Paul was writing had in all probability nothing in written form to guide them other than these letters.

From our vantage point it is hard to imagine a time when Christians didn't have the four Gospels and an entire New Testament. But that was precisely the situation with Paul's Thessalonian readers. All the gospel they had was what Paul and his fellow missionaries had given them orally in Thessalonica and these two letters.

You will recall from studies in the book of Acts that Paul and his associates took the gospel to Macedonia during their second missionary journey. First, they landed at Neapolis and then traveled the few miles inland to Philippi. And after establishing a small group of believers there, they moved west along the Egnatian Way approximately ninety miles to the Aegean port city of Thessalonica.

Paul, under the guidance of the Holy Spirit, was a master strategist in selecting Thessalonica as a center for Christian activities. The city's population in the middle of the first century was about 200,000. It was the capital city of Macedonia and a major center on the Egnatian Way, the Roman road that connected Rome with Constantinople—modern Istanbul. From this major center, the Christian message could travel east or west on the Egnatian Way or across the Aegean Sea by way of the many ships that moved in and out of the harbor.

Paul's ministry in Thessalonica produced powerful results, and a church was established. However, as you will remember, the hostility of the large Jewish community was so great that Paul and his missionary associates were forced to leave the city because of the threat on their lives. They traveled approximately thirty miles west to Berea where they had a successful ministry until some of the troublemakers came down from Thessalonica and created such an uproar that Paul hurried on south to Athens and from there to Corinth.

During the time Paul was in Athens, though, he sent for Timothy and Silas who had remained behind in Berea. After consultation they sent Timothy north to Thessalonica to see how the young church was getting along. By the time Timothy returned, Paul and Silas had moved on to Corinth, so they got the report there.

Paul heard that the Christian community in Thessalonica was thriving. At the same time, though, Timothy told him that some problems had arisen in connection with the teaching on the Second Coming of Christ and how Christians should conduct themselves while waiting for that event. It was this report that prompted Paul to write his first letter.

It is possible that either Timothy or Silas returned to Thessalonica with the first letter and spent some time there. Then, either they or someone else reported back to Paul that conditions had not improved following the first letter. The confusion centering around the return of Jesus was still a serious issue. On one hand, there were those who believed the Event had already occurred while others were still involved with their bad and inappropriate behavior.

It was this persistent confusion that occasioned the second letter. Here the tone is less relaxed and personal, and Paul goes into considerably more detail on the Second Coming of Christ. And in both letters Paul is dedicated to building up his readers' faith through a clear and expanded understanding of God, of Jesus Christ, and of the

Holy Spirit, while at the same time relating this teaching to the practical business of living each day for the Lord.

There is also a positive word for us in the twentieth century. We have the promise that Jesus is coming again—we don't know when. Speculation is not the important issue. But it is important that we live each day with a creative and Christ-like style.

Preface

The Apostle Paul stands in the setting of Christian history as one of the greatest personalities of all time. If Protestantism had a patron saint, it would have to be the zealous converted Jew from Tarsus. Indeed, all traditions of Christianity recognize that in the unique man Paul, God called a missionary thinker who has scarcely been surpassed in his ability to define clearly the issues of the Christian faith.

Paul, the Apostle.

This Paul was no armchair theologian. He was hardly divorced from the experiences of people or their suffering. Indeed, he himself was whipped and imprisoned in Philippi. He raised a dead man at Troas and caused a riot at Ephesus. He was called a god at Lystra and finally was martyred at Rome. Paul was a genuine man of God, but he was every bit flesh and blood. He was an incredible missionary statesman, but, as we will discover, he had a tenderness that continues to touch us today. He truly learned what it meant to be a loving and faithful follower of Jesus.

By God's wisdom and grace it was this man's letters that became a significantly large part of the Holy Scriptures that we study as a means to wholeness of life. There is an order to the books of the Bible, but we need to recognize that the way the New Testament has been organized was

Paul's Letters.

not the order in which the letters of Paul were written. Instead, for our understanding and study it may be helpful to have Romans at the front of the Pauline letters because that book deals, in a comprehensive manner, with becoming and living as a Christian. But we may miss something very important if we are fuzzy about what issues or what letters started Paul on the road to his becoming the most famous letter writer of all time.

Thessalonians and the Order of the Letters.

Hidden almost at the end of Paul's writings in our New Testament are the two little letters to the Thessalonians. Many Christians scarcely know what is in them, except perhaps that these letters contain some ideas about the end of time and hope after death. It may be that their emphasis on the end of time is the reason these letters were placed near the end of Paul's writings.

The collectors or organizers of the letters thought in a systematic fashion. They started with the salvation letters —Romans, Corinthians, and Galatians. Then came the letters dealing with Christ—Ephesians, Philippians, and Colossians. Next, they added the letters dealing with final things—Thessalonians, and they concluded with letters addressed to individuals—Timothy, Titus, and Philemon.

This biblical organization is excellent, if you wish to think systematically. But if you want to think historically, it is not Romans but the Thessalonian letters that were among the earliest. We are not quite sure about the dating of Galatians, but with the possible exception of that letter, our study of Thessalonians has us reading Paul at the beginning of his letter-writing career.

Dating Thessalonians.

The Thessalonian letters were probably written from Corinth very soon after A.D. 50. As Luke indicated in Acts 17, Paul had been forced out of Thessalonica and then out of Berea by hostile Jews. He left Silas and Timothy in northern Greece (Macedonia) and journeyed south to Athens and on to Corinth. According to Acts 18, he was later joined in Corinth by both Silas and Timothy and then stood trial before Gallio, the Roman proconsul (governor) of southern Greece (Achaia).

Fortunately, we can come quite close to dating this experience because the tenure of a proconsul was usually one or at most two years in an area. The Delphic Inscription suggests that Gallio probably arrived in Corinth on the first of July, A.D. 51. Paul likely came to Corinth in A.D. 50, and 1 Thessalonians was probably written during the early part of his eighteen-month stay at Corinth (Acts 18:11).

The Thessalonian letters, which emerge out of that traumatic period in Paul's life, have been greatly loved by Christians of all time. Not only do they deal with one of humanity's greatest concerns—death and the end of time—but these letters also provide a very tender portrait of a caring and concerned missionary. In the Thessalonian letters, it's evident that Paul desired wholeness and stability for all his Christian friends in the struggling churches in Greece and Asia Minor. To read the Thessalonian letters is to gain a glimpse into the heart of Paul, a person who became a model of Christian life and mission.

Concern of the Letters.

In a quarter of a century of teaching seminary students of many different denominations and in various settings throughout the world, it has been my desire to help them understand that the New Testament writings are not to be seen as merely ideas. Through the power of God's Spirit these writings may be experienced as truly living words of comfort, hope, encouragement, and challenge from real servants of God who were the early followers of "the Way." It is my prayer now that you, as you study, may be helped to feel the pulse of Paul. As you meditate on the words of this apostle to the gentiles, I trust that you will be captivated by his heart and mind, as I have been.

A Personal Word to Readers.

Remember throughout this study that you are probably reading some of the earliest words preserved from the pen of Paul and of the entire New Testament. Watch for germinal ideas that Paul developed into more complex statements. But most of all, read these letters in an attitude of prayer that the caring spirit of this young missionary on his second evangelistic journey might touch you as it touched the Thessalonian Christians in the first century.

LESSON 1
1 THESSALONIANS 1:1—10

A Respected Church

Dear Lord, Open my heart to hear and receive what You have for me in this lesson. AMEN.

As we begin this lesson, let your mind drift a little and imagine that for a few moments you are back in the time of Paul and are visiting in Thessalonica. Macedonia, in northern Greece, had a great heritage. From this region of the world came Philip of Macedon. The city of Krenides was renamed Philippi after him. Philip was the father of Alexander the Great, recognized by many as the greatest general in the history of the world. Alexander had begun his illustrious life in the palace city of Pella just a few miles east of Thessalonica.

After Alexander's death and the division of the empire among his generals, Cassander, Alexander's brother-in-law, succeeded in gaining control of the northern part of the kingdom, which included Macedonia. On the banks of the Axios river where it enters the Thermaic Gulf, Cassander founded a new capital in 315 B.C. and named it for his wife, Thessalonike. The selection of that site by Cassander was superb and the city began its long history.

After Macedonia fell to the Romans in 146 B.C., Thessalonica (Thessalonike) was designated a Roman colony and the capital of the Roman province of Macedonia. Eager

Paul's Salutation to the Thessalonians (1:1)
Thessalonica.

17

to connect all parts of the empire to Rome, the Romans built one of their famous interstate roads through Macedonia, linking the Adriatic Sea with Turkey. At the heart of this Egnatian Way stood Thessalonica. The Apostle Paul came to this city early in A.D. 50 by way of this Roman road (Acts 17:1).

Persecution at Thessalonica.

Not much is known about the church at Thessalonica during the early period apart from what is in the New Testament. But we do know that the people of Thessalonica had a very strong attachment to the cult of Rome, and coinage has been found from the Augustan period bearing the inscription of Caesar as "god." From this we know that the stage had been set for a major conflict between Christianity and the worship of Caesar.

Although the Christians at Thessalonica had been the object of persecution earlier, it came with full force in the time of Diocletian and Galerius (ca. A.D. 303–311). Galerius, one of Emperor Diocletian's four lieutenants (sub-emperors), selected to assist in the reestablishment of Roman traditions and the rooting out of Christianity, was headquartered at Thessalonica. And it was here that he built a massive triumphal arch on which he is pictured as seated among the gods. He also added a magnificent mausoleum in which he was to be buried.

At the death of Diocletian, Galerius assumed the primary title of Emperor and continued the terrifying persecution until he was killed in A.D. 311. As a strange twist of history, with the peace for Christians that followed the death of Galerius, the mausoleum was transformed into a memorial for Christian martyrs.

But that event was not to be the end of persecution for Christians in Thessalonica. After the fall of Constantinople in 1453, Macedonia came under Turkish influence and Christians there suffered an Islamic persecution. This situation was not reversed until the twentieth century when in 1913 Greece finally regained control of Macedonia.

Today, although a number of cities of ancient Macedonia lie in ruins, Thessalonica has survived as Salonika, the second largest city in Greece. Its survival has something to say about Cassander's knowledge of site selection. Yet we must also reflect on the fact that the early Christians had laid a solid Christian foundation so that even the ruthless Galerius could not destroy Thessalonica's Christian testimony.

The story of Thessalonica and this church's later sufferings are not unrelated to the concerns of the Thessalonian letters. Here we are dealing with a church that almost immediately after it was formed experienced the trauma of persecution at the hands of jealous Jews (Acts 17:5–9). The concern for the life to come with God was raised at the very beginning of this church's existence. To live effectively with expectation can become the spark for igniting a great church. To misdirect or reject that expectation can be a cancerous experience that eats at the very heart of a church.

As we study these letters together, we will discover both rejoicing for strength in Christian living and encouragement for continued growth. We will also find warning against inappropriate views of the Christian life and the future. In our first lesson the focus is on encouragement and growth.

Focus of the Letters.

Both 1 and 2 Thessalonians open with a form of address that is typical for writing a letter in Paul's time. It reminds me of the way inter-office memos often begin today, except that the name or names of those sending the letter are mentioned first. The simple form for the Greek letters is "X to Y. Greetings." The form may be expanded so that X or Y may include various titles or more than one person or organization. The greetings may also be greatly expanded to include a variety of good wishes or appropriate greetings. For an example of a complex opening, see Romans 1:1–7.

In the Thessalonian letters the simple names are used. Here Paul is joined in writing the letters by Silvanus and Timothy. There is no doubt, however, that Paul is the primary writer and even though he frequently uses the first person plural, "we," he does revert to the first person singular in several places, such as: "I charge you" (1 Thess. 5:27) and "I write" (2 Thess. 3:17). We don't know how much the other two members of the team added to these letters.

Opening Form of the Letters.

It is clear that Silvanus is the Silas who became the companion of Paul after the separation of Paul and Barnabas (Acts 15:40). Silvanus/Silas apparently was a trusted member of the Jerusalem Church (Acts 15:22) and like Paul seems

Silvanus.

19

to have been a Roman citizen (Acts 16:37). We know from other references that Silas worked jointly with Timothy in Berea (Acts 17:13–14) and in Corinth (2 Cor. 1:19; Acts 18:5).

Although we cannot be absolutely certain that the Silvanus who was the scribe for Peter (1 Pet. 5:12) is the same person as the Silvanus here, it could well explain his function as a scribe for Paul. From the text of 2 Thessalonians 3:17–18 it could be argued that Paul actually wrote in his own hand only the concluding greeting and that Silvanus served the secretarial role here just as Tertius did when Paul wrote to the church at Rome (Rom. 16:22).

Timothy.

Timothy, the junior member of the team, is usually better known to most Christian readers than is Silvanus. According to Luke, he was probably from Lystra in southern Galatia and was the son of a Jewish-Christian mother and a Greek father. Apparently he was already a believer by the time of Paul's second mission journey to Galatia (Acts 16:1–3). Two letters in the Bible were addressed to him, and from 2 Timothy it could be inferred that he was a third-generation Christian, since Paul spoke of knowing the faith of both his grandmother, Lois, and his mother, Eunice. Paul then added that he was confident that such faith was present in Timothy as well (2 Tim. 1:5).

Timothy is mentioned in several other letters of Paul as his "beloved son, and faithful in the Lord" (1 Cor. 4:17) and as his son in the gospel who was known by his service and caring for others (Phil. 2:19–23). Paul apparently had great confidence in young Timothy and seems to have used him consistently as his messenger and personal envoy (1 Thess. 3:2–6; 1 Cor. 16:10–11; and Phil. 2:19–23). It is intriguing not only that Timothy is viewed in 1 Thessalonians as one of the writers, but that his movements from place to place also form part of the content of the letter itself (1:1 and 3:1–10).

The Idea of Church.

The Thessalonians are addressed in these letters as a church. The Greek word *ekklesia*, meaning "assembly" (a compound word originally meaning "called out"), soon came to be the Christian's technical word for the gathered community. But Paul makes it clear to his readers that this gathered community has its origin or basis not in human activity but in God's call.

It was easy then, and it is now, for churches to forget

On Paul's Second Missionary Journey, while he was traveling from Philippi to Thessalonica, the capital city of Macedonia, he traveled through Amphipolis. The "Lion of Amphipolis," pictured here, was a prominent landmark in Paul's time and was located right along the road on which Paul probably traveled. The lion was erected in the early part of the fourth century B.C. to commemorate a victory.

their divine origin and think and act as though they grow and develop by human ingenuity. Certainly we are all called to work diligently for Christ, but at the same time the words of Charles Wesley are most appropriate: We need to work for God as though everything depended upon us; but, we need to pray and trust as though everything depended upon God.

The God of the Church.

Paul also spelled out the divine nature of the Church when he wrote that it depends for its existence upon "God the Father and in the Lord Jesus Christ" (1:1). This statement of dependence is in fact a great *confession.* We learn that from the very beginning, when Christians experienced the resurrection of Jesus, they realized that He was to be identified with God.

The term "Lord" was an affirmation of divinity, in both Jewish and Greek thought patterns. When the Romans insisted that the people in the empire call Caesar, Lord, most of them responded patriotically. They had many gods; what was one more?

But the followers of "the Way," Christianity, became a major political problem because they refused to recognize and accept anyone as "Lord" but Jesus Christ, who was at one with God.

Christian Greetings.

The brief salutations of both Thessalonian letters reached a climax in the significant Christian greeting, "grace and peace" (1:1). You will remember, I am sure, that the typical Semitic (Jewish, Arabic, etc.) greeting is "peace" (*shalom, salam,* etc., from which comes the familiar place name Salem). It is also interesting to note that the Greek greeting *chairein* ("greetings") and the Greek word *charis* ("grace") have a common root. Paul's habitual use of this greeting would have had significant meaning to his first-century readers.

Although scholars are correct that the combination greeting "grace and peace" is related to an Old Testament idea of "mercy and peace," I am convinced that the early Christians must have seen something incredibly more important than a rehash of Jewish ideas in their greeting. Any Greek-speaking Christian would quickly recognize the similarity of their words of address to the two earlier greetings. But they would also realize that even in greeting one another, Christians were saying something about their faith to the two great ancient cultures.

Indeed, the order of the words forms a significant confession because Christians are not merely witnesses of peace to the world but are also proclaimers of the grace in Christ Jesus that leads to peace. People of all time have been searching for peace. But Christians who truly live out the meaning of this greeting have a message to the world that the foundation for peace is grace—the gift of God!

I wonder sometimes if we don't need to be as creative as the early Christians were in their greetings. What does "hello" or "hi" mean to us today? And how do we address and conclude our letters? Are our greetings truly Christian or simply secular?

After concluding his salutation, Paul usually opened his letters with a thanksgiving prayer. Only in Galatians, where he was disturbed with the heretical tendencies of the Christians in Galatia, did Paul fail to begin with a thanksgiving statement.

In this first letter the prayer of thanksgiving for God's marvelous work among the Thessalonian Christians is actually a single complex sentence in Greek that includes all the remaining verses of chapter one. Actually, though, Paul was so grateful for the faithfulness of his friends in Thessalonica that his heartfelt attitude of thanksgiving continues all the way through chapter three.

From Paul's words early in this letter (1:7–8) it becomes clear that the reputation of the Thessalonian Christians for faithfulness and devotion to Christ was widely known. In fact, Paul tells them that the good news about their Christian life and witness has not only spread throughout all of Greece but to the Christians all over the world. It is quite remarkable that in just one year the church in Thessalonica had become an example and model to churches everywhere. What a testimony to the power of God!

One way or another, though, as Christians, our lives are a witness, an open book ready to be read by others. We may fool ourselves and a few other people at times, but our life patterns tell others who and what we really are. Our manner of life often provides the open door for witnessing and the opportunity for doing more in the name of Jesus. It is

Paul's Prayer and Grateful Reflections Concerning the Thessalonians (1:2–10)
Thanksgiving.

The Thessalonian Reputation.

23

important, then, that the lives we live conform to the gracious model of our Savior.

Good News/Bad News.

We often hear that "bad news travels fast," but God can make good news travel quickly as well—that is, if we are really interested and want to hear good news. Unfortunately, though, most of the time people are interested in bad news, and that is one reason newspapers and television reports are filled with death, destruction, failure, and crime. Bad news sells newspapers, and we buy bad news.

The God of Thanks.

But in this case the good news about the Thessalonian Christians' faithfulness had deeply moved Paul and his team. And so we read that the missionaries gave "thanks to God always" for them (1:2). Paul was always sensitive to the need to affirm his Christian brothers and sisters in the Lord, but at the same time he knew that it was God at work in them that produced faithfulness. And for this, he praised God with a thankful heart.

It is so easy for us to get mixed up in the matter of praise. We are all very human and like a pat on the back. In fact, God knows that we all long for a hug and want to be told that we are important and that we count. There is nothing wrong with that. But we must be always mindful that ultimate praise and recognition belong to God.

Paul did not make the mistake that tempts many Christians. He knew who was the source of goodness and power, and his references of thanksgiving to God were not merely polite attempts at humility. He knew that any praise for his own accomplishments, and those of the Thessalonian Christians as well, belonged to the Lord.

Christian Virtues: Faith, Love and Hope.

Paul now goes on to affirm his readers for their Christian virtues of faith, love, and hope (1:3). We are familiar with this triad because of its appearance in the thirteenth chapter of 1 Corinthians. It is quite likely these three virtues were widely recognized very early in the Christian communities. They may indeed have been considered a kind of summary of the exemplary virtues of the Christian life.

The most familiar order for this triad is faith, hope, and love (1 Cor. 13:13; Rom. 5:1–5; and 1 Pet. 1:21–22). But the order in 1 Thessalonians (1:3 and 5:8; also Col. 1:4–5) has an important and logical progression that seems to be related to the pattern of salvation. Although these three virtues certainly apply to all stages of the salvation process, notice the order: (1) a special emphasis on "faith" is often made in reference to becoming a Christian (justification); (2) "love" may be the element most exemplary in living as a Christian (sanctification); and (3) "hope" is the quality most evident in the Christian's expectation of the future life with God (glorification).

Stages of Christian Life.

It will be helpful at this point, I believe, to think of the theology of the Christian life in three stages. In doing this, I am reminded of the story about a well-known British Christian who was approached on the street by a zealous believer who asked, "Brother, are you saved?"

He responded by saying "Yes! Partly! and No!" His "yes" meant that he was truly justified, made right and acceptable to God by faith. "Partly" meant that he was in the process of being sanctified—not perfect, but seeking to live the life of love. And the "no" meant that he was not yet glorified for he hadn't gone to heaven or experienced the great hope of the hereafter.

Certainly, as Christians, one of our most important tasks is to gain a better understanding of the marvelous breadth that is encompassed within our great words for salvation and for the Christian life. I believe that many of the problems of definition existing between denominations would be significantly eased if we could learn how to accept the breadth in the biblical words and recognize the contribution which each church and tradition offers to our overall understanding of salvation.

Factors in Their Christian Lives.

After introducing briefly in his opening words the fact that the Thessalonians have evidenced the qualities of Christian life, Paul now moves on to remind them of certain truths that have contributed to their development as Christians. He begins at the crucial point. In order for us to understand salvation and the Christian life we must start our thinking *with God*, not with people.

God and Election.

In verse 4 Paul reminds his readers that they are loved by God and are numbered among His chosen or elect people. Unfortunately, many people stumble over such words as "election" or "chosen" because of the tendency to define them in an exclusive and deterministic fashion. Much harm has been done in Christian thought by arguments

The Arch of Galerius was built after Paul's time (A.D. 330). However, it straddles the Via Egnatia over which Paul traveled from Philippi to Thessalonica. The street is still an active thoroughfare in modern Thessaloniki, which is today the second largest city in Greece.

such as: If some are chosen, obviously God has rejected others. It is genuinely questionable whether Paul would have taught such a negative determinism. His primary concern here is for Christians to recognize the marvelous loving act of God in their election as His children.

The great evangelist of the nineteenth century, Charles

Spurgeon, who loved to use the term *elect*, was able masterfully to go beyond the narrow determinism of some Christians when he prayed, "God save your elect, and then elect some more." God's genuine desire is that no one should perish, but that all should come to new life in His Son (see also 2 Pet. 3:9).

Paul and the Gospel.

For Paul, the evidence of the "election" of the Thessalonian Christians was their acceptance of his missionary preaching (1:5–8). The apostle reminds them that "our gospel came not unto you in word only, but also in power, and in the Holy Ghost" (1:5). His preaching was more than words because God took those words and surrounded them with the transforming power of the Divine Presence. The Thessalonians were convinced that it was not merely Paul who was speaking to them, but that it was God who was touching them through Paul and those with him.

Paul identified the content of his preaching as the "gospel" (*evangelion*). The strict meaning of the Greek word for gospel is good news, as when a runner brought the good news of a victory against the enemy. But the word *gospel* in Christian circles soon became known as a technical term for the Good News concerning salvation in Jesus Christ.

For Paul and the early Christians, the Good News was that in Jesus Christ the Old Testament promises of a coming Messiah had been fulfilled, and that although Jesus had done nothing but good, the jealous Jews had put Him to death on a cross. But God refused to allow evil to be victorious and raised Jesus from the dead. This was the message that all Christians were expected to share with others (see also Acts 10:34–43).

And so we understand that the Good News is a testimony about Jesus and His transforming power. It has been made available to everyone by God through the coming of Jesus. I am emphasizing this basic Christian truth here, even as Paul did for his Thessalonian readers, because it is important that we understand that our Christian witness and testimony concentrates on Jesus and not our humanness. Unfortunately, many testimonies today often emphasize the sinful condition of people prior to their becoming Christians. In fact, some people seem to think that the worse sinner you *were*, the better your testimony will be. But such testimonies are usually not a glorification of Jesus but of evil and of the self.

When Paul spoke of "our gospel" (1:5; see also 2 Thess. 2:14 and 2 Cor. 4:3) or "my gospel" (Rom. 2:16), he did not mean that the gospel was about himself. Paul was not Paul-centered. What he meant was that the message he was presenting was his testimony about life in Christ Jesus. And that message about salvation through Jesus was not merely powerless talk—"in word only." Rather, it was alive in him and his companions through the Holy Spirit—"in power, and in the Holy Ghost" (1:5).

Christian Modeling.

Paul then acknowledges that his readers joyfully accepted both the testimonies and the lives of Paul and his companions as exemplary messages that came directly from God to them through the work of the Holy Spirit (1:6). And by following their example the Thessalonian believers became models or examples of what it meant to be Christians to many others both in northern (Macedonia) and southern (Achaia) Greece and in "every place" (1:7–8).

Imitation.

This pattern of copying an example or model Paul called "imitation." In the Western world the idea of imitation frequently carries a negative connotation because we usually think of it as the opposite of genuine. But neither Paul nor the Greek educators of that time held that view. For them, imitation was viewed very positively. A good teacher was one who made it possible for students to copy or imitate him.

The attitude was similar in Jewish culture. A great rabbi was one who could get students to pass on to others traditions and interpretations without change. Accuracy of transmitting traditions without variation was the sign of a good student, while independence of thought was reserved for the few who had achieved a certain stature.

When Jesus called people to "follow," they understood that the Lord meant they should try to copy or imitate His way of life. That's what it meant to be a disciple or learner. Paul frequently called for imitation and, as he indicated in Philippians 3:17, not only did he want people to imitate him, but he encouraged churches to watch for people in their congregations who were also worthy of imitation.

Today, however, we have become much more word-oriented, and we often judge people's Christianity by whether or not they *say* the things we think they should. At the same time we are hesitant to suggest that people should copy us because we are worried about not measuring up to the standards we would like to have for ourselves. Our "humility" is admirable, but our hesitancy to be models is hardly worthy of praise.

Modeling the pattern of Jesus, however, cannot be accomplished by mere human will, as Paul clearly acknowledged in verses 5 and 6 of our Scripture lesson. It takes the presence and power of God's own Spirit to become an authentic model of the Christian life.

The Basis of Modeling.

The reason that such modeling is so important is that authentic Christian lives are the best proof that the gospel works; it is the best bridge-structure to the non-Christian world. Our lives as Christians are bridges that God uses to touch and influence our families and neighbors—in our town and across the world. It is God alive in us that witnesses to His presence and power.

Then, too, it was apparently the way the Thessalonians handled pain—"much affliction"—that caught the attention of the world. They accepted the gospel joyfully in spite of the pain, trials, or the afflictions that it caused them. The Greek word *thlipses*, translated as "affliction" in verse 6, does not mean some little concern. Rather, it suggests the kind of trial experienced in persecution.

Suffering and Modeling.

We've already seen that the church at Thessalonica was known throughout Greece, but of great importance was that its reputation was based on the consistency of its faith and behavior (1:8). Paul didn't have to tell others that the Thessalonians had given up idol worship (1:9). That transformation was obvious. Anyone who knew them also knew that the old Greek gods no longer meant anything to them. They were not fence sitters trying to live with two patterns of life at the same time. They made a decision to live for Jesus and to serve the only true God, and it cost them plenty in terms of suffering.

The Thessalonian Testimony.

One of the most significant things that happened to the Thessalonian Christians was that in their suffering their understanding of God came alive. They became living witnesses of what they believed. And they believed that in Christ there was an answer to the bitterness that fre-

A Living Theology.

29

quently comes with the pains and hurts of life. Although not every problem had an immediate resolution, they believed that in Christ there was a resolution to their problems. For this reason they were able to be patient in their pilgrimage of faith.

Paul's words in verse 10 give us rare insight into the thinking and attitude of the Thessalonian Christians: "And to wait for his Son from heaven, whom he raised from the dead, even Jesus, which delivered us from the wrath to come." They were ever alert to the return of their resurrected Lord, and that expectation became the theme of their lives. The anticipation of seeing Jesus, the Son of God, Who would appear from heaven and deliver them from God's judgment upon the wickedness of the world, was more than enough to compensate them for the difficulties and suffering they were experiencing for their faith.

The Coming Wrath.

The judgment, wrath, and anger of God are ideas that were never popular and they aren't today. There is a widespread notion, although not necessarily expressed in so many words, that God is forever ready to get us out of trouble and that He is some type of sugar-daddy who will supply our every want. Believe me, the people of Israel knew from hard experience that such a picture of God was hardly realistic.

Although the God of the Old Testament was not a soft touch, Israel knew that He most certainly was not an impulsive, angry God like the gods of their gentile neighbors. He was a God of covenant love, and His nature was to love and forgive. But at the same time the Israelites knew that He was not to be treated lightly. God's anger or wrath was not unjust, haphazard, or enigmatic like some human emotions. It was seen or felt only when His chosen people rejected His loving care.

In the New Testament the primary term for the wrath of God is *orge* and its frequent linkage with words like "righteous" (see Rom. 2:5) indicates that it is a determined effect that lacks any similarity to unbridled human anger. To understand the wrath of God we must visualize it in the context of the rejection of God's love. That is the plain meaning of the great wrath passage in Romans 1:18–32. God may be loving, but He was not playing a game with humanity when He sent His Son to die for our sins. There is justice in this world even though at times it may seem to be delayed.

But of one thing we can be sure: At the end of time as we know it, there will be judgment upon all of sin. The day of the Lord's coming will not bring joy and rejoicing to everyone. To many people the day of the Lord, as Amos indicated, will bring darkness and not light because that day will be a day of dark regret and mourning (Amos 5:18). To face the reality of God and His Son, Jesus, the Christ, means to take very seriously both the possibility of life with God in the resurrection and the possibility of judgment because of sin.

The Thessalonian Christians knew beyond any shadow of a doubt that their God was alive. They didn't need statues of Him to be reminded of His presence. Unlike the pagan gods of their neighbors, their God had made Himself known in a truly unforgettable manner through the resurrection of Jesus from the dead. That irrefutable fact is the hinge point of Christianity. It is the guarantee of our faith, and it is the basis for our hope in the future. Without it there would be no Christianity and we would still be in our sins and without God.

The Resurrection.

But because Jesus was raised from the dead, we, like the Thessalonians, can have a future irrespective of any present difficulties and pain. We, like the Thessalonians, can in the power of the Holy Spirit become imitators of Jesus' pattern of life and models of Christian integrity. And we, like the Thessalonians, can reject the fence-sitting techniques of those who take the name "Christian" but find it difficult to let Christ transform their relationships in this world.

Our Challenge.

In the opening words of this remarkable letter Paul has given us a revealing picture of a group of first-century Christians and of a virile church fellowship. They were the talk of the Christian community throughout all of Greece because of their commitment to Jesus Christ. But theirs was no cheap commitment for it demanded not only words of witness but also actions and behavior in witness.

We late-twentieth-century Christians like to think of ourselves as quite advanced and sophisticated. Yet from what we've seen in this lesson, those first-century Chris-

31

tians from the northern Aegean port city of Thessalonica can be examples for us now. Their clear faith and action-packed piety is a model with world-changing potential.

Lord God, Help me to live the Christian life empowered by the Holy Spirit, walking in Your presence, doing only the things that You have called me to do. AMEN.

WHAT THIS SCRIPTURE MEANS TO ME
—1 Thessalonians 1:1–10

In 1959 our six-year-old son, Carl, died from a terminal blood disease. Before his illness I was disinterested in religion and completely indifferent to the God of the Universe.

That tragedy caught me with an empty faith bucket. During the three months of Carl's illness I tried desperately to come to know the God who heals. But when Carl died I felt betrayed and lapsed into anger and bitterness. Consequently, I did my grief work badly and spent a long time living in the black quagmire of grief and depression. Through God's patience and faithfulness, the faith of others, and my own weak prayer, "Lord, help me to love You more," He began to heal my brokenness. With His help I was able to walk slowly out of the blackness back to color, and light, and life.

It wasn't long after my experience with the Lord that my husband, Chuck, entered the seminary to prepare for the ministry. After spending fifteen years in the business world, this was a dramatic move for us both. But with my recent experiences of God's reality and Chuck's confidence in His call, we moved with shared anticipation into our new life-style with feelings of invulnerability.

The seminary proved to be a spiritual desert with a scarcity of watering holes! As babes in Christ, we found those years to be painful and difficult. We both struggled, in different ways, over the apparent lack of concern for spiritual matters and a disdain for Christian fellowship.

One professor sagely predicted that in five years the institutional church would be obsolete! Often, our beliefs seemed to be discounted or simply ignored, and we felt very much alone.

Those explosive years of the early 1960s were filled with social action flags and "God is dead" proclamations. They were disturbing days, but happily, now that same seminary has a spiritual vigor and a balanced approach to the Christian faith that bears little resemblance to those times.

But even as those early Thessalonian Christians were buoyed up and encouraged by Paul, Silas, and Timothy, we, too, found encouragement during our seminary days from our Christian friends. In answer to Chuck's letter expressing his concern over the humanistic climate of the seminary, The Rev. Sam Shoemaker, revered rector of Calvary Church, New York, for many years, quickly replied, "Thank God you came into the ministry on the wave of an experience, not just an idea."

During those times that Chuck seemed overwhelmed by a spiritual drought, I suggested periodically that he visit the Rev. Dr. Charles King, a spiritual giant in the Presbyterian church in our city. Chuck always returned from these visits with a new joy. When I asked, "What did Dr. King say?" Chuck's answer was usually some version of "I can't remember exactly what he said. It's what he is and what he stands for—his faith and commitment—that's the important thing."

Just as Paul sent Timothy to visit and remind the Thessalonian Christians of the joy and the hope in the gospel, and of the promises and power of the Holy Spirit, we, too, were sent friends who encouraged us in the Lord. And, in that alien seminary atmosphere, I desperately needed their encouragement and their reminders of God's goodness and faithfulness. On my better days, I could remember The Story, and hold the assurance that "Jesus is Lord." On other days, however, my faith waned and was about as stalwart as a wet noodle. How I needed my enablers!

I don't recall a Timothy or a Silas standing on our front porch ringing my doorbell, but these friends must have been related to those early Christians, for they said basically the same things. And, after a good visit, one last hug, and a promise to lift us in prayer, they reminded us of who we were and Whose we were. And while they always brought us some extra portions—like a pot roast, fruit, sugar cookies, pecans—to help us stretch our meager budget, they left behind something far more valuable—the faith, joy, love, and hope of the Lord. How like Paul's words of hope and affirmation to that small group of Thessalonian Christians who were also living in an environment that was alien to their faith and convictions!

LESSON 2
1 THESSALONIANS 2:1—3:10

A Caring Servant

Father, Make me into a true servant. Help me to serve others because there is a need to be met; not for recognition, and not from guilt or obligation, but for Your glory. AMEN.

Paul's Style as an Apostle (2:1–12)

A Spirit of Love.

The verses included in this lesson contain some of the most forthright yet tender statements written by the Apostle Paul in any of his letters. Christians who have pictured Paul primarily as a harsh disciplinarian or a rigid, doctrinaire person need to breathe deeply from the spirit of the apostle in these verses. Unlike some Christians today who use words such as *love* and *caring* as facades for our aggressive, imperialistic manipulation of others, the apostle to the gentiles really had a heart of love.

For the most part, I believe Christians want to live lives of love. But love and respect can so easily become a thin veneer to which we give lip service but little else. Then there are those who use love as a sledgehammer in order to make others conform to their desires. There may be a great deal of talk about love, but their hearts are still far from it.

This was not the spirit of Jesus and wasn't the attitude of Paul. Jesus died in genuine love for us, and Paul modeled that same spirit. We must always remember that the whip in the temple was only a very tiny part of the story of Jesus. The symbol of our Lord was not that of a whip, but of a cross.

The crusades, the Inquisition, and the witch trials of colonial New England were shameful eras in Christian history. I happen to believe that it is not beyond the realm of possibility that some variation of that pattern could become a reality today. It is not at all beyond the stretch of our imagination to believe that we are seeing the political, social, and psychological ingredients beginning to emerge that could produce another series of human disasters in the name of Christianity. Self-protectionism of religious people has become a soaring worldwide phenomenon. We can see this tendency not only in Christianity but also in Islam, Judaism, Hinduism, Sikhism, Buddhism, and other of the world religions. For this reason, it is important that we become increasingly sensitive to the times in which we are living and try to learn from the caring spirit of the Apostle Paul.

The Way of Dialogue.

Paul was in dialogue with the Thessalonian Christians in what we know as chapter two of this letter. And dialogue is not merely talking; it also involves listening, not simply pausing from talking in an impatient manner until someone else finishes so that we can begin again.

Unfortunately, so much of what we might label as dialogue is only a series of slightly related monologues in which people are not really listening to one another. It is even possible at first glance that we might think Paul is just giving a long monological defense of his ministry in this letter. But that is not the case. Paul was an excellent listener, and this is what made him a superb teacher. He really gave his attention to what others said. Paul was always genuinely interested in other people—not primarily for his own sake but for theirs and for the sake of God's work in the world.

Paul and His Critics.

Paul opened this part of our Scripture lesson by referring to the basic motives in his own life. There is no doubt that he was a successful missionary. The Thessalonian Christians were living testimonies to his success. Some Jewish enemies and perhaps even certain Christian critics were probably jealous of this success. They may even have tried to stir up the Thessalonian converts by accusing Paul and his companions of trying to get economic and political gain out of winning people to their teachings.

But Paul could not let a charge like that go unchallenged because that would have undermined everything he stood for. And so as he responds to that criticism in this lesson, we are privileged to get an intimate look into his heart and mind.

Gain or Pain.

In response to any questions his critics may have raised, Paul readily acknowledged that his coming to them had hardly been empty or unproductive (2:1). They knew this, but they also knew that if Paul were in the business to make a profit or obtain people's praise, all the critics needed to do was to take a good look at his life. It would become obvious quickly that he was hardly out to make a "quick buck" from the gospel. Instead, the gospel had already cost him a great deal of pain (2:2).

In making his point in this second verse, Paul did not list all the personal abuses that he had sustained. Other experiences could easily have been added, such as those found in the book of Acts—the assassination plot in Damascus, persecution in Psidian Antioch and Iconium, and the stoning at Lystra (Acts 9:23–24; 13:50; 14:5, and 14:19).

But Paul didn't have a self-centered martyr complex. His purpose here was simply to counter the idea that he and his companions were self-centered by pointing to something the Thessalonians knew firsthand—the imprisonment and beating they had experienced at Philippi just before going to Thessalonica (2:2). The truth was that their motive for preaching the gospel was authentic, self-giving obedience to God.

It is important for us to remember that suffering for Christ still goes on even in the twentieth century. Many Christians have died for the cause of Christ in Third World countries. Others, even in North America, have suffered economic and psychological abuse in standing up for the principles of Jesus. We may be considered soft and castigated for refusing to pad contracts or to fudge on our income tax. I've known men and women who risked their jobs for not taking unfair advantage of customers or clients.

Let's face it, it is possible that if we love people in the

name of Christ, it may raise hostility among our unchristian associates and friends. But now, as in the first century, the Lord will use, in some way, our difficulties, hard times, and suffering for His purpose and glory.

Paul now moves on to explain their style of presenting the missionary message, "For our exhortation was not of deceit, nor of uncleanness, nor in guile" (2:3). The Greek word translated here as "exhortation" is *paraklesis*. It is related to the familiar "paraclete" (*parakletos*) or "comforter" that is used often of the Holy Spirit in the Gospel of John.

The Missionary Style.

It is Paul's intention here, I believe, to remind his readers that his message to them had been one of encouragement, appeal, and comfort. He wanted them to understand that he and his companions had come to them as agents of God and caring ministers who wanted through their life and witness to make a difference in the lives of the people in Thessalonica. Paul and his fellow missionaries were so convinced of the authenticity of their Good News about Jesus that they desperately wanted their Thessalonian friends to experience the new life in Christ.

Although their appeal (exhortation) had been strong, Paul makes it clear in verse 3 that they refused to compromise the integrity of their gospel message in an effort to win followers. Because their message came from God, they were convinced it was authentic and was not the result of any faulty human effort.

Integrity.

Then, too, Paul makes it clear here that their message was absolutely uncompromising in its demand for moral purity. And at no time would they capitulate to easy patterns of deceptive advertising or misleading promises in order to win converts. For Paul, the end never justified the means.

There is a most practical lesson for us in these words of Paul. As Christians we are to witness to what God has done for us in Jesus Christ. But Paul is saying here that we are never to compromise the integrity of our witness in any way in order to "win" someone. We are not to manipulate the thinking and emotions of people in our evangelistic efforts. And above all, like Paul, we are to refuse to "play to the galleries"—say what others want to hear in order to look good. Our task is to be authentic witnesses; it is the task of the Holy Spirit to do the convincing. And as far as Paul was concerned, it was God's approval on his life and message that really counted (2:4–6).

I firmly believe that now, as in the first century, there is an openness to the Good News. Hollow people are searching for answers because of the desperation of the times in which we live. They're not looking for slogans but for something that really works and will give meaning to life. This is precisely why our witness and our actions, to be effective, must conform as much as possible to the simple and direct message and actions of Jesus, who was never manipulative or devious.

One's Impression of God.

There is another very important truth that comes through to us in verse 4. Paul knew the God he followed and worshiped, and he knew that God approved of his ministry of service. His encounter with God through Christ was intensely personal. Here, indeed, was the source of Paul's wholeness and power.

Unfortunately, too many people have a hazy impression of God. Many people's god is the god of their father and mother, or the god of a book or of a particular set of rules, the god of a certain experience or of a feeling. For others, their god is the god of a preacher or teacher or place. But these kinds of gods usually leave people feeling empty and not satisfied.

As important, though, as rituals and rules may be, it was the personal encounter Paul had with Jesus that made the difference—that changed him from a rule follower to a Christ follower. For Paul, God was no longer just an idea or a set of rules. God had become a Savior and Lord whom Paul understood after meeting Jesus. There was nothing vague or abstract about his God, even though, like with us, there was no way in this life Paul could fully penetrate the mystery of God.

Approval and the Living God.

Paul discovered a living God and was concerned about living *with and for* that God. He lived with and sought to please the God who in Christ lives in the hearts of believers. And God became a living companion for Paul and approved of him (2:4) because of his effort to conform his life to the pattern of Jesus (see Phil. 2:3–11).

God was Paul's approving agent. Most of us strive for

38

human approval even though we know that it is usually very temporary—almost as whimsical as a crowd at a baseball or a football game who cheer for a player one moment and then boo him the next.

Because conformity to Christ was Paul's chief goal in life and because everything in his life required God's approval, Paul refused to flatter or exploit people for personal gain (2:5). He was so sure of his basic goals in life that he even summoned God to witness to his integrity in a kind of mock court scene: "God is witness" (2:5).

There is an important lesson for us in Paul's words and example here—exploiting or manipulating other people is not the pattern Jesus gave us. And, certainly, Paul, who never hesitated to claim his role as an apostle, refused to use the privileges of apostleship for his own ends or gain (2:6). Indeed, so great was his concern not to be a financial burden to his newly won followers that he worked to support himself (2:9).

Finances and the Missionary Way.

In this personal confession (2:6, 9) Paul set out an important perspective on the missionary pattern of the church for Christians of all time. As I have indicated elsewhere, I believe that when the church moves into new regions with the gospel, it is important that missionaries not be dependent for their support on the people to whom they are ministering. Such a pattern frees missionaries from appearing to non-Christians (who might not understand their message) to be gaining financially from their work.

The message of Christ's love and forgiveness should never appear to be offered for sale. Such a pattern is totally foreign to the Good News about Jesus Christ. We are not salesmen or peddlers of God's gospel (see 2 Cor. 2:17). Rather, we are witnesses to His goodness and love in sending Jesus to the world for our salvation.

But this does not mean that we, as Christians, are free of responsibility for the financial support of pastors and missionaries who have been called to special service in the church. Nor does it mean that we are free from the responsibility of witnessing wherever we can to God's wonderful love. The responsibility for sharing the gospel with others rests on everyone who has experienced the power of God's forgiveness (see Phil. 4:15–20; 1 Cor. 4:12; and Acts 20:31–35).

Two Colorful Pictures.   Paul followed his personal confession about finances with two extremely tender word pictures that are windows into the heart of the apostle.

In the first picture, Paul compared himself to a nurse whose life is consumed in caring for children (2:7). He didn't want to be viewed merely as an itinerant evangelist or philosopher who didn't care about people and was concerned only with dispensing words of great importance before moving on to another place. Even though his time in Thessalonica had been cut short by Jewish persecutors (see Acts 17:1–10), Paul wanted the Thessalonian Christians to know that his care and concern for them was like that of a nurse or a nursing mother who invests herself in the lives of the children in her care.

Indeed, the picture of the nurse may have suggested itself to Paul because he was forced to leave the Thessalonians so soon after they had experienced the new birth and were still not really able to be on their own. Like a caring nurse or mother, Paul wanted them to realize that he not only wanted to share the gospel with them, but that he was eager to share his very self with them, "because ye were dear unto us" (2:8). Here again, Paul gives us a model for Christian witnessing—we are to open ourselves up in love for others. This involves much more than merely putting a few dollars in the offering plate on Sunday morning.

In the second picture, Paul compared himself to a concerned father whose children needed the counseling and advice of a wise and caring parent (2:11). But first he reminds them in verse 10, without any appearance of boasting, that he is qualified for his role because he has lived a just and holy and blameless life before them.

In making that rather astounding statement, Paul certainly wasn't claiming that he had lived a perfect life. Actually, to understand just what Paul meant here we have to remember that he was brought up as a first-century Jew and intepret his words in the context of his time. What he was actually saying here is that he believes God approves of him because of the kind of relationship he has with the Lord and with other people. It wasn't that he was perfect, but that he was accepted by God. He didn't mean that he was as good as God, but that he felt secure enough to say, "I'm O.K." in the Lord.

Paul then goes on to remind his readers of God's call and expectation for them: "That ye would walk worthy of God, who hath called you unto his kingdom and glory" (2:12). While Paul had affirmed his parental role with his Thessalonian friends, he reminds them that the source of their salvation is God and he and his associates are merely His servants.

God's Call.

We learn from Paul's words here that he recognized his proper place and that he did not make the common mistake of humanity—trying to be like God. In the Garden of Eden the temptation of Adam and Eve was to be like God (Gen. 3:5). Humankind's consistent problem has been in trying to prove, as one of the Russian cosmonauts, that God is not what He says he is and that people know how to run the world better than God does.

Paul and the Human Mistake.

But Paul knew that he was not God—not even a little god! His goal in life was to help people discover that Christianity was not some imprisoning opiate or drug, as Karl Marx later thought, but that Christ was the greatest liberating power in the world.

Now, as Paul reflects on how the Thessalonian Christians had discovered the transforming reality of Christ, he launched into a prayer of thanksgiving (2:13; see also 1:2). He thanks God here for their positive response to the gospel. But what is so heartwarming about this second prayer of thanksgiving is the way Paul's humanness comes through. He didn't pretend that he had the power to be an alter ego for God (another form of God) so the world would see that when he spoke, he was obviously the mouthpiece of the divine. That may be the way some people think about Paul, but that image is entirely false. What we discover here is the human Paul who is extremely grateful to God that his Thessalonian friends were able to see that God was communicating with them through the words of very human missionaries.

A Great Thanksgiving (2:13–16)
Paul's Thankful Spirit.

At the same time Paul knew that even though his message was important because it came from God, commu-

ABOVE AND RIGHT. Thessalonica was an important commercial port in Paul's day and was also the home of a naval base. Located on the north end of the Aegean Sea, and as a port of entry for the capital of Macedonia, the harbor teemed with ships in the first century— even as it does in the twentieth century.

nication is a two-way process—people have to be ready to listen in order to receive a word from Him. And Paul understood that it was God who had prepared the Thessalonian Christians to hear and receive the truth.

It is this kind of humanness and sensitivity to the dynam-

ics of the Spirit at work in a two-way communication that
has made Dr. Billy Graham's preaching and ministry unique
and effective.

As Paul continued his reflections about the Thessalonian Christians, he returned to the theme of imitation and
modeling that was introduced in the first lesson (2:14–15;
see also 1:6). The reference here is to the suffering and persecution that his readers were going through. Paul draws
the comparison between the kind of persecution experienced by the Christians in Palestine and that of the Thessa-

Imitation and Suffering.

lonians. Both were suffering pain and persecution because of their faith in the Lord Jesus. But their response had not been bitter or vindictive. Rather, the Thessalonians, like their Jewish counterparts, had followed the model of the reconciling and self-giving Christ.

Paul Condemns the Opposition.

In this part of our Scripture lesson (2:14–16) Paul speaks out with uncharacteristic harshness against the Jewish persecutors who were creating so much trouble in the church at Thessalonica. The intensity of the opposition there on the occasion of Paul's first visit (Acts 17) was white hot. And it was this same kind of opposition that plagued Paul and his Christian friends at every turn.

This opposition had to be terribly disconcerting, but the amazing thing we see here is that although Paul's anger was strong toward the Jewish troublemakers, he resisted taking matters into his own hands by striking back. I have the feeling that while wrestling with this crisis, Paul had a message from God. And it was a message that served him as well then as it did later, when he wrote to the Christians at Rome, quoting Deuteronomy 32:35, "Vengeance is mine; I will repay, saith the Lord" (Rom. 12:19).

There is no doubt that Paul felt a sense of righteous indignation over those who were trying to stop the gospel witness. But he also understood that his persecutors and those of the church were merely building a case against themselves with God and that they would have to face His wrath (2:16). In other words, Paul turned his opposition over to God.

There is a powerful application for us in Paul's attitude and actions here. So often we take matters into our own hands because we're unable to see the big picture of God in our world. Most of us act as if our God is too small to handle problems in the church and society, so we try to be "little saviors" and set things right ourselves. But, unfortunately, our actions are usually out of harmony with God's way and purposes. Not so with Paul—his task was to preach the gospel. He left the opposition in God's hands.

Paul's Desire for Another Visit (2:17–3:13)
The Grieving Parent Picture.

Having completed his discussion on those who were persecuting him and the church, Paul returns again to his personal relationship with the Thessalonian Christians

(2:17). He now pictures himself as a grieving parent who has lost a loved one. Although the expression of loss we see here may not seem to us to be as permanent as death, Paul paints the word picture he does because he wants his readers to understand the intensity of his feelings. He loves them and misses them desperately. And his memory of them burns like a fire in him as he longs to visit them again.

Once again, through his words here, we catch a glimpse of a very tender and caring Paul. The love he felt for his Christian brothers and sisters ran very deep. He knew so well that the Christian faith cannot be lived in isolation. Rather, it is enlivened and enriched through fellowship with other Christians.

The Enemy and Paul.

Paul next acknowledged the ongoing battle with Satan, whom he says had put obstacles in his way to seeing them. Although the personification of evil in a figure like Satan—the adversary—was a little hazy in the Old Testament, by New Testament times he was clearly seen as a personal figure who had dominion over the realm of darkness and who was the ultimate reality opposed to God, Jesus, and the Holy Spirit (2:18).

For Paul, there was nothing vague about the presence of evil in the world. It was in fact a stark reality that was opposed to his mission of spreading the Good News of Jesus Christ. The battle against evil is ever present with all of us. And as Martin Luther is supposed to have said, "If you don't believe in the devil, it's because you've never tried to resist him."

Paul's Expectation: Christ's Coming in Power.

But in spite of the enemy's work, Paul knew that Satan was not the ultimate force in the universe. Christ had won the battle against evil through Calvary and the empty tomb. And although Paul was separated from his friends in Thessalonica and was always engaged in a battle against evil, he was looking ahead to the final glory of the "Lord Jesus Christ at His coming" (2:19).

The Greek word used for the coming of the Lord is *parousia*, which has its roots in the Greek verb that can be translated "to be present." The meaning here is that at Jesus' future coming—His *parousia*—He will come in power. And it is then that the true nature of the commitment to Christ by the Thessalonian Christians would be obvious to everyone. Their hope and joy and crown of victory was tied to Christ's *parousia*. And their faithfulness to the gospel was most certainly Paul's "glory and joy" (2:20).

We get the feeling from Paul's words here that he is very proud of the Thessalonian Christians and their relationship to Jesus Christ. He had been with them when they had found the Lord. He was their spiritual mentor and guide. And now his joy in seeing their faithfulness and growth can be felt as he writes them. In a similar way, I believe that our challenge as witnessing Christians is to become spiritual mentors to others. This same joy can be ours as we see Christ at work in the lives of our friends and neighbors.

Timothy's Visit.

Paul next reminds his readers of Timothy's visit to Thessalonica, and he tells them that he sent Timothy "to establish you and to comfort you concerning your faith" (3:2). Paul knew they needed this support because of the persecution and affliction they were undergoing for their Christian commitment (3:3). Even though when Paul had been with them earlier he had warned them that they would experience persecution and be tempted to abandon their faith, he knew the subtleties of their temptation and was anxious about them (3:5).

But then Paul hurried on to tell them that when Timothy returned from that visit, his good report about their faithfulness and devotion was comforting and encouraging to him (3:6–7).

A Troubling Question.

Some people are bothered by Paul's anxiety and worry about the well-being of the Thessalonian Christians. Their thinking runs something like this: Why was Paul so concerned about them if they were really Christians? Such a question seems to imply the idea that they should have been safe from temptation because they were Christians.

But Paul was understandably concerned. These were new Christians who were being severely tested. He knew from personal experience the power of Satan, and he was prepared to risk his own welfare to help them "stand fast," or to be secure in the Lord (3:8).

Paul's Challenge to Us.

Paul then winds up this part of our lesson with a joyful expression of thanksgiving for them as he again writes of his great desire to see them.

Paul has in this particular lesson given us an indelible model of what it means to love and care for the people around us and across the world. With all of the sophistication of our twentieth-century technology, millions go to bed hungry every night, others are oppressed because of the color of their skin, and still others live under unspeakable conditions of physical and mental suffering. At the same time millions feel the stress of being out of work, of being alone and without any kind of hope for a life with meaning.

And even today, there are Christians who must remain "underground" and who go through all kinds of hardships because of their faith. Although the form of opposition may be different from what the Thessalonian new Christians experienced, spiritual, mental, and physical suffering is very much a reality as we read our newspapers and view reports on television.

As with Paul in the first century, we twentieth-century Christians are called to care and pray and act. The great apostle modeled for us the strategy for our service to others as he lived out the example of Jesus, "Even as the Son of man came not to be ministered unto, but to minister, and to live his life a ransom for many" (Matt. 20:28).

Heavenly Father, Thank You for the religious freedom this country allows. I appreciate the abundance of Bibles, good Christian literature, and Bible-based churches that dot our landscape. Thank You for Your great mercies and provision. AMEN.

WHAT THIS SCRIPTURE MEANS TO ME
—1 Thessalonians 2:1–3:10

My friend surprised me with a question, "Since we are leaving on vacation, will you keep my valuable jewelry?" With no hesitation I replied, "Absolutely not! Store them in a safety deposit box. I don't want to be responsible!"

In today's lesson Paul speaks of God entrusting us with His gospel, something far more valuable than the family jewels. Accepting the gospel of salvation can be life changing. And being willing to share the Good News can, sometimes, be frightening. And knowing the best way and the right time to share the gospel is not always obvious. Each opportunity is unique, and it helps to be prepared by earning the right to speak.

When our oldest daughter entered college, I went to work as a receptionist and switchboard operator in a large store. For years I had been living very protectively under the "umbrella" of the church, so I was unprepared for the store's secular environment.

My co-workers were indifferent toward the Christian faith and suspicious of me, a minister's wife. Not only did my "God words" have no currency there, but I sensed they might bring alienation instead of fruit. So I decided to try to be the best receptionist I could and to be a supportive, caring friend to my fellow workers. It was my hope that if any crisis erupted in their lives, they might ask, "Carolyn, how do you handle the fearful scaries in your own life?" Then, I could tell my own faith story.

Becky, a fellow employee, and I often shared coffee breaks. Unknown to me, she had grown up in an anti-church environment. As the song in the musical, South Pacific, so aptly concludes, "You've got to be carefully taught." And she had been very carefully taught to distrust God and Christian people. After we got better acquainted, I learned that she hadn't been too happy about a preacher's wife being hired to run the switchboard. She had expected me to enter the store rattling my cross and spouting Scripture! Instead, we just laughed together, shared some special moments, and became friends.

After working in the store for about six months, my phone rang one night, and through tearful gulps, Becky said, "My husband has asked for a divorce. Can you come over?" When I arrived at her house, her first words were, "I am so lost!" With a silent prayer for guidance, I listened, and then began to share with her God's faithfulness in my own desert experiences.

After a time I asked if she would like to try a prayer experiment. Assuring her that she could begin with just a fingernail's worth of faith, I told about the "Thirty Day Prayer Experiment" we learned from Dr. Sam Shoemaker. I explained that for thirty days she and I, separately, would pray for God to be present with her at the point of her greatest need—her marriage. We wouldn't presume to tell God what to do about it, but would just turn the relationship over to Him.

Becky refused, insisting she really didn't believe in prayer. "All right," I answered, "but if you're still in that pit, and you get down to your last rope—God's rope—just call, and you're on."

About three weeks later, she telephoned. Tearfully, she said, "I guess I'm down to my last rope!" The prayer experiment began. Becky's marriage ended, but her faith blossomed and matured.

For years now, Becky has been a committed Christian, and an active member of our church. With a smile on her pretty face she says that sometimes she wants to grab folks and shout, "Please, let me tell you about God!" But, as she remembers her own fear of someone doing that to her, she knows to wait for God's time and opportunity.

Now, when I see Becky in church on Sunday mornings, I understand a little bit more about Paul and how joyful he must have felt as he thought about those beloved Thessalonian Christians whom he led to Christ. Paul's faithfulness to God and the love he showed toward his friends in the Lord are models for each of us in our own pilgrimage of faith.

LESSON 3
1 THESSALONIANS 3:11—4:12

Paul's Call To Love and Holiness

Abba Father, Lead me in Your way of holiness and Your way of love. AMEN.

Paul's Signal Prayer (3:11–12)

Prayers in the letters written by Paul are always very significant. They are usually found at the beginning of the letters (cf. 1 Thess. 1:2– 10; Rom 1:8–15; 1 Cor. 1:4–9, and so on) and indicate Paul's sense of gratitude to God for the Christian believers. On the other hand, when prayers occur in the middle of a letter, they form a kind of spiritual summary of what has been written before (cf . Eph. 3:14–21), while at the same time alerting the reader to pay particular attention to what follows. At times they serve as marks of transition.

The prayer that opens this part of our Scripture lesson (3:11–12) is a captivating transitional statement. It not only includes mention of Paul's passionate desire to return and visit his friends in Thessalonica (3:11), it also summarized his great desire for them to "*abound* in love one toward another, and toward all men" (3:12, italics mine). The idea expressed here by Paul is that they were to "overflow" with love toward others; they were to be full and running over.

Doing God's Will.

Paul, as we have seen through our studies, was a God-directed person. He lived with the firm desire to do God's will and to obey God's leading in the everyday activities of life. Paul's commitment to God was constant; it didn't surface only in times of crisis and special need. Rather, he was always careful to seek the will of the Lord even in such ordinary and routine matters as whether to make the trip from Athens to Thessalonica. His primary desire was to do God's will instead of merely doing what he wanted—a sure mark of growth in Christian maturity.

Living in Love.

In this prayer, we see that Paul not only prays for personal guidance about when he might visit them, he also directs his attention to their great need—the need to love, the mark of a genuine Christian life (3:12; cf. John 13:34–35 and 1 Cor. 13). And we also sense his deep longing for his Thessalonian friends to not only express Christian love in their relationships to each other and to everyone else but to demonstrate it (3:12). Indeed, Paul's prayer was that love would pour forth from them like a spring or geyser that could not possibly be contained. And, once again, Paul sets himself up as a model for them to imitate, "even as we do toward you."

Paul understood our natural tendency to only love those who love us or to only love people who are like us in color, economic status, and religious understanding. But the love Paul experiences and writes about goes way beyond racial identity, social status, or spiritual position and includes everyone. And so he prays that they will copy him in his overflowing love for them.

We, like Paul's first-century readers, have much to learn from his words here. We find it easy to nod our heads in agreement when we are urged to love one another. Words come easy, but it was actions that counted with Paul. It is one thing to "talk" love, but it is quite another thing to "act" love. And yet, love, as John reminded us, is shown and felt by the way we act (1 John 4:7–21).

The First of Paul's Practical Instructions (3:13–4:12)

Paul's brief prayer here (3:11–13) signals the transition to the practical instructions he wanted to give his readers on how they should live as Christians. You will recall that in some of Paul's other letters he opened with a teaching or theological section and then devoted the rest of the letters to practical instructions.

In 1 Thessalonians the transition from the teaching section to practical instruction is suggested when the prayer for love in Chapter 3:12 becomes a prayer for acceptable holiness in Chapter 3:13. In other words, when Paul focused his attention on holiness he was beginning his instruction on how the Thessalonian Christians ought to live.

Love and Holiness in Salvation.

Now it is important at this point that we remain very clear on the matter of salvation. For Paul, Christian love for others flowed from God's love in Christ for us. Genuine love for others is the authentic garden soil of life that our master gardener, Christ, can use to produce the fruit of true holiness. Like the vineyard keeper who pruned the branches in the beautiful metaphor of John 15, Paul pictured the Lord here as one who was working on Christians to strengthen their hearts—their whole person—so that they might pass the test of life.

Throughout these Thessalonian letters Paul and his associates insist that a person does not earn salvation because of works or holy living (also Rom. 3:28 and Eph. 2:8–9). Instead, we come to God by faith. How we act—how we demonstrate our faith, is exceedingly important at the time of "the coming of our Lord Jesus Christ with all his saints" (3:13).

Paul's Concern for Holiness.

The Greek work for holiness in verse 13 is directly related to the word for sanctification that appears further on in Chapter 4:3. However, it is important for us to understand that when Paul wrote that they should be "unblameable in holiness," he didn't think that they would be perfect in any mathematical sense of perfection, anymore than he thought he himself was as perfect as God.

Actually, Paul's thought here is similar to John's—in Christ, Christian believers have become clean or pure (John 15:3). I believe Paul's mention of them being "unblameable" refers to his desire for the Thessalonian Christians to be acceptable to God, free from guilt. Put another way: He wanted them to realize that they were okay as far as God was concerned.

Then, too, I believe that Paul wanted his first-century readers to remember that while our holiness is the result of God's holiness in us, it is our duty to act and live like accepted daughters and sons of God. This is a recurring theme through all of Paul's writings—our actions are to be living witnesses of God at work in us as we in love serve other people at the point of their deepest need.

A marvelous late-twentieth-century picture of this kind of holiness and love is seen in the simple and self-giving life of Mother Teresa of Calcutta. She didn't win the Nobel Peace Prize and capture the admiration of people throughout the world merely by profound statements or inspired rhetoric. Rather, she is respected and loved because she has put her Christianity to work among the poor, the sick, and the dying in the slums of the world. Blaise Pascal was right when he wrote, "The serene beauty of a holy life is the most powerful influence in the world next to the power of God."

As we move to the conclusion of this prayer now, we see that Paul has placed all Christian activity in an eternal setting—the second coming of Christ (3:13). Apparently he had a heavenly courtroom scene in mind here as he visualized the coming Jesus being surrounded by His "holy ones." Our King James text reads "his saints." Many leading Bible teachers today are most likely correct in regarding these not as human saints but as heavenly beings or angels.

The Coming of Christ and Christian Life.

The scene here reminds us of the earlier visions of God in which He was surrounded by thousands of angels (see Deut. 33:2). Undoubtedly, Paul is identifying the coming of Jesus with the Old Testament picture of the Day of the Lord (also Zech. 14:5 and Dan. 7:10). The unity of Scripture and the way Paul draws on Old Testament references and truth highlights the eternal consequences of all Christian activity.

Once again, Paul's teaching has important implications for us even as it did for his first-century readers in Thessalonica. As Christians, the way we are living has serious implications for the future, for the eternity that lies beyond what we know now. Paul knew so well that everything we do—our Christian behavior in relation to our neighbors across the street or across the world—is a part of our being ready and prepared for the Lord's coming.

Paul's prayer, which we've just studied, provided a powerful introduction to an advice part of his letter which begins now (4:1) with some very practical instructions in living. These were important to Paul, and we shouldn't treat them as an appendix to his teaching. He knew that it was not only what one believed that was important.

Believing and Living.

Equally significant for him was how Christians applied their beliefs to the way they lived.

Unfortunately, many Christians today cut their Christianity off from the issues of life. They seem to think that *believing* alone makes them Christians. It is this kind of person who can glibly quote Ephesians 2:8–9 on being saved by grace alone but conveniently forget what follows, "For we are his workmanship, created in Christ Jesus unto good works..." (2:10). For Paul, believing and doing (or living) were two inseparable parts of truly being a Christian. To focus on one without the other is to make the Christian gospel either an empty philosophy or a powerless way of life.

Paul's Concern for Conduct.

Because Paul knew firsthand the incredible importance of Christian conduct, he opened Chapter 4 with a double-pronged appeal. To emphasize the intensity of his feeling and meaning he uses double verbs, "we *beseech* you, brethren, and *exhort* you..." (4:1, italics mine). Paul is being very emphatic here as he moves into this instructional part of his letter. Once again he reminds them that they are to live in a way that pleases God, even as he had taught them when he was with them in Thessalonica (4:2).

The urgency of Paul's appeal seems to indicate that while Timothy had brought him a good report on their growth in the faith, it is also likely that part of his report caused the apostle some concern. Paul was always sensitive to the fact that the new gentile Christians were scarcely a heartbeat from the paganism of the Greek world. He knew the power of the temptations that could shake them as they moved through the routines that were a part of their culture. And so we have to feel that there were good reasons for him to focus first on the subject of sexual license.

Sexual License in Paul's Day.

Sexual freedom and license were a general hallmark of gentile morality in the first-century world. Ancient Greek philosophers like Demosthenes made it clear that men needed "prostitutes for pleasure...mistresses for the day-to-day needs of the body...wives for the begetting of children and for the faithful guardianship of our homes."

There was little stigma associated with sexual promiscuity, but it was not the privilege of both sexes. Instead, it was the recognized and accepted life-style of the male members of society, and officially run houses of prostitution were established to bring money into local and state treasuries much like lotteries and pari-mutuel betting are today. The idea was that if people were going to do certain things, they should be legalized and taxed. Sounds familiar, doesn't it?

Then, too, as we've seen already in our studies, temple prostitution was common in the pagan worship of that time. In Thessalonica this form of worship was practiced by the cult of the Cabiri of Samothrace.

It was to people living in the middle of this culture that Paul wrote the words in this part of our lesson (4:3–5). As a Christian, he was committed to moral integrity. The teachings of Jesus and the early church made it clear that sexual activity was to be restricted to marriage—to a lasting and monogamous marriage.

Paul and Holiness in Living.

It is important for us to note that Paul opened his instructions on sexual morality by making it clear that the will of God for them was their "sanctification" (4:3). This is a somewhat technical biblical term for holy and pure living. Paul then followed this call to holy living with a series of instructions focused on sexual morality. But it is important for us to understand that by moving so quickly from mention of holiness to sexual morality Paul did not mean that holy living should be defined *merely* in terms of sexual activity.

It would be easy to misread Paul at this point. I've been with groups of Christians from time to time who seem to define sin primarily in terms of sex, and they make a big point of insisting that sexual sins must be publicly confessed. At the same time, though, not much mention is made of such sins as gossiping and lying and cheating. But a careful study of Paul's instructional sections in each of his letters indicates his insistence that sin is sin irrespective of the form it takes.

In this letter, however, it is likely that Paul focused immediately on sexual morality because of a particular problem and need within the Thessalonian church. We've already seen something of the culture in which these new Christians lived. And the pressures for them to revert to their former sexual worship practices and general gentile morality patterns must have been very strong.

Thessalonica society must have thought that these new Christians were a pretty weird lot because of their strict life-style. But Paul was careful to remind his readers that they were now very different from their pagan neighbors "which know not God" (4:5). And I'm sure it was as hard to be "different" in first-century Thessalonica as it is for us in our twentieth-century world. The pull is always for conformity. But Paul reminded his readers that there is no room for sexual impurity in the life of the Christian (4:7).

Practical Instruction.

Paul's instructions in verse 3 are very direct and precise: "abstain" from all inappropriate sexual relations. Our King James text reads "abstain from fornication," but Paul's Greek term included all forms of immorality.

We see a parallel here to what Paul wrote the Corinthian Christians, "*Flee* fornication...he that committeth fornication sinneth against his own body" (1 Cor. 6:18, italics mine). Paul understood the power of the sex drive, and he knew that the only answer was to *run away* from any and all temptations of deviant and improper sexual behavior.

Once again we see that more than 1,900 years of "human progress" has not changed some things all that much. While it is true that most of us are not assaulted by pagan worship practices that involve immoral behavior, we are subjected to "forms of entertainment" that would have appealed to the pagan sexual morality of first-century Greece.

As Christians we need to give as much attention to *running away* from improper sexual involvements as we do to jogging, walking, and contemporary health concerns. We face a moral wellness crisis, and the health of all Christians and of our society is at stake. The time is right for a firm Christian moral stand now even as it was in Thessalonica.

The Christian Under Control.

Immediately following his stern warning to run away from immorality, Paul makes an important statement, "That every one of you should know how to possess his vessel in sanctification and honour" (4:4). A few translations of this verse interpret the word "vessel" as "wife." But I firmly believe that our King James text is correct. Nowhere in the New Testament is a person ever regarded as the "vessel" of another person. Rather, Paul's instruction here is that we are to gain control or mastery over our own "vessel"—body—in holiness and honor.

As Christians, our bodies are to be brought and kept under control. They are vessels meant to be used as God intended—in holiness and honor. We are not to be like the gentile pagans Paul wrote about in Romans 1:18–32, who refused to honor God and instead dishonored their bodies by practicing all kinds of improper sexual activities including homosexuality. It is clear here and elsewhere that Paul labeled all forms of immorality as sin, and the fact that such behavior was accepted by first-century Greek society did not change his thinking at all.

I'm sure it was true then as it has been in the centuries since Paul wrote his letters of instruction to those early Christians that there were those who believed Paul was unenlightened and rigid because of his insistence that the gift of sex was to be enjoyed only in marriage and was not something to be misused and abused. Paul knew that the teachings of Jesus and the popular gentile morality of his time were totally incompatible.

Paul's insistence on sexual purity has profound meaning for our twentieth-century culture. While forms and styles of sexual immorality may differ somewhat in their expression today, the blatant flaunting of Christian values can so easily anesthetize our sensitivities that instead of "running away" we "look the other way." For Paul, there was no hint of compromise. We are to possess our bodies and conduct ourselves before the Lord in holy living.

Building Faith and Trust.

Paul next gives us his third exhortation in this instructional section (4:6). The Christian is not to defraud, take advantage of, cheat, or "go beyond" his brother by invading personal and private boundaries. Some teachers of the Bible have thought that in saying this Paul had shifted his attention from sexual to economic morality.

While I am sure that there can indeed be an application of what the apostle is saying to economic morality, I believe he has still something very significant to say about sexual morality that applies to Christians and the church. The church, as Paul saw it, is a close and intimate community of people. In such a community, faith and trust are absolutely essential. But even as within a marriage, if someone in the church strays across set boundaries by becoming involved sexually with another person, faith and trust within the community are shattered. Neither in family life nor in the fellowship of the church can we violate trust relationships without unleashing disruptive forces that threaten the unity and spiritual life of the entire community.

When I was growing up, I attended a fairly large urban church that was almost like a family. There was a sense of family trust that gave everyone a feeling of security. For anyone to have violated the individual and family boundaries would have wreaked havoc within our community of faith. We trusted each other, and that faith and trust was guarded carefully. As members of the body of Christ, implicit faith and trust in each other is essential to our spiritual health.

Paul's Thesis.

Next, Paul reaches his major thesis on Christian behavior, "For God hath not called us unto uncleanness, but unto holiness" (4:7). This theme can be both a goal and a warning because it calls us to live Christ-centered lives that are pure and holy, and it reminds us that this business of being a Christian is serious.

Our Picture of God.

Unfortunately, though, I believe that a softness has invaded the late twentieth-century church, at least in the Western world. This may have occurred because we seem to have developed a fluffy picture of God. Not only is our "god too small," as pictured by Dr. J. B. Phillips in his book with that title, but that god is as spineless as a melting snowman.

Most of us tend to picture God in our own image rather than allow the Bible to form our portrait of Almighty God. Nowhere in the Bible do we find a God that is weak and uncaring. Rather, the God of the Bible and the God and Father of Jesus our Lord is very concerned about all of our thoughts and actions. And most certainly, the God of the Bible opposed sin so much that His Son came into our world to settle the matter of sin once and for all through His life, death, and resurrection.

God's Purpose.

God's purpose for us is to live obedient and holy lives in the world today. Jesus didn't enter our human history to organize another club called the church. He came to found a new society of believers in Him who are committed to

Excavations of arched buildings in Thessalonica, which date back to first-century times. These were undoubtedly busy shopping centers.

living out the teachings of Jesus in the nitty-gritty of to-day's world. And the warning in verse 8 is unmistakably clear as Paul writes that anyone who ignores this teaching is in fact rejecting God Himself.

As members of God's body, the Church, we are meant not only to witness but to *be* witnesses in the office, in the marketplace, in our homes, to the Good News of life in Christ even if it means confronting head-on the immoral forces at work in our society.

Love in Community.

Paul next moves in his writing from instructions on sexual morality to his readers' love relationship with each other as members of the Christian fellowship (4:9–10). The Greek word that Paul uses for love here is *philadelphia*, a term originally employed in reference to members within a family. But the term soon came to include a relationship within a community.

The early Christians saw themselves as a family. They needed each other and were drawn together in love as they worked to live Christian lives in a hostile environment. It was this spirit that prompted the early Quakers to name their city Philadelphia. Their environment, too, was hard and often hostile, and they knew that their faith could only be strengthened and enlarged by drawing together in love and concern for each other as members of the family of God.

And it is this spirit that can enliven and energize Christians today. Our mobile life-style tends to break down the sense of family within the church. But as Christians in a hostile environment—an environment stained by violent crime, threat of nuclear contamination and war, irresponsible acts of terrorism, and relaxed moral standards—we desperately need each other. It is only as we are drawn together by the Spirit and love of Christ that we can make a difference in our world. The watchword for us as Christians is "philadelphia!" It is this genuine caring and not bitter divisiveness and name-calling—infighting—that will cause people around us to want what we have in Christ.

Taught of God to Love.

It is intriguing, I believe, to note that in Paul's teaching here he moved from a topic of inappropriate and erotic love (4:3–8) to a reminder of the need for genuine Christian love and caring for one another. And while the shift from one topic to another may seem a bit abrupt to us, it was typical of Paul's style in giving practical instructions to his readers. As a rule, his instructions did not involve long statements but were a collection of short pieces strung together like a string of pearls.

In a similar fashion now as Paul writes about brotherly and community love, he doesn't discuss in extensive detail all that is involved. Rather, he affirms that they are already "taught of God to love one another" (4:9).

The term "God taught" in this verse is unique in that it appears nowhere else in the New Testament. And from its use here, it is obvious Paul believed that God had been working in the hearts of his Thessalonian friends. He could see this through the quality of their family and community love. And of great importance was that their concern and love for one another was not limited to their own particular fellowship, but included as well their brothers and sisters in the Lord throughout all the province of Macedonia (4:10).

At this point the Christians in Thessalonica provide us with a model greatly needed in the church today. It is not the Christian pattern to look out for and love "only our own." Rather, the Jesus model and the Thessalonian model calls for including in our caring community people from all across the world. The poor, the hungry, the have-nots wherever they live are our concern and responsibility.

Encouraging and Discouraging Activity.

While Paul complimented his readers for their spirit of caring and love and community, he challenges them in verse 10 to an even greater awareness of their need to expand this loving spirit—"that ye increase more and more."

Paul understood clearly that life is a process. There was that constant need for encouragement to develop and sharpen their good qualities. But then in verses 11 and 12 he makes reference to certain negative qualities that needed to be firmly discouraged.

At first, we may wonder at the connection between Paul's instructions in verses 11 and 12 with brotherly concern and love. But it is apparent that the three things he mentions here were a hindrance to their witness as loving and caring Christians. And so Paul closes out this part of our lesson with some extremely practical advice.

"Study to Be Quiet."

We are not certain precisely what had been reported to Paul that caused him to give this bit of advice, "study to be quiet" (4:11). It is possible there were those who were gossiping or making critical remarks about their fellow Christians. These are temptations that have plagued Christians of all time. Talk can take on some very cheap and destructive forms. As children we used to chant, "Sticks and stones can break my bones, but words can never hurt me." That is so wrong! Words do hurt and wound terribly.

At the same time there may have been those in Thessalonica who were aggressive and tactless in their witnessing and Christian testimony. This can so easily drive people away from church. But whatever the problem, Paul knew that silence can at times be a powerful and healing force in community life. Silence, under certain circumstances, may well be the strongest sign of "philadelphia"—community love.

"Do Your Own Business."

Next, Paul urges his readers to mind their own business (4:11). These words speak volumes! Apparently, the Thessalonian Christians were not only a loving and caring people, but it is possible that at times they carried their concern to extremes and became busybodies.

Paul knew that meddling did not build a sense of community, harmony, and well-being. The love and fellowship he has been writing about in this letter must not degenerate into nosiness or a blatant invasion of privacy. Brotherly love and caring respects the rights and dignity of others.

"Work with Your Own Hands."

Paul's third gem of advice urged them "to work with your own hands" (4:11). In the gentile world of the first century working with one's hands was generally considered degrading, a lower-class activity fit only for a slave. But involvement in work wasn't the reason Paul wrote as he did here.

Apparently, some of the Thessalonian Christians were guilty of not working for a living because they were convinced the Lord was going to return almost immediately. They used the *parousia* as an excuse for loafing and not working. This meant, of course, that they were a burden to others—and that is a sure way of disrupting any feeling of love and community.

Paul and his fellow missionaries had always been careful not to be a burden to their Christian friends. It was for this reason that he often refused to accept a subsidy from his churches and made his own way with the tent-making trade. To impose on the generosity of others is diametrically opposed to the spirit of Christian love and community.

Christians in Glass Houses.

These last three pieces of practical advice were extremely important in maintaining a spirit of love and community among the Christians. But there was also wise counsel here in the relationship between the Thessalonian Christians and their non-Christian friends and neighbors. Apparently some of them were getting a bad reputation among the non-Christians for their noisy, meddling, and nonproductive life-style. Sometimes Christians may be a hindrance to the gospel. Even today we've heard some people say, "If that is what Christianity is all about, I don't want any part of it."

We who profess to know and follow Christ do live in glass houses. Others—Christians and non-Christians alike—look to us as examples of Christ's message of forgiveness and love. In this lesson Paul is calling his readers of all time to an authentic holiness of life and love that will enable us even in the midst of our very human pilgrimage to live a life of adventure in Christ and to influence others to share in our experience.

Our task—yours and mine—is to live as useful, creative, and productive members of society in the neighborhood, town, and state in which we live. We are not to be merely verbalizers of the Good News of Jesus Christ but effective and influential living representatives of that gospel.

Father God, Let me be an example of the believer in word, in conversation, in love, in spirit, in faith, in purity. AMEN.

WHAT THIS SCRIPTURE MEANS TO ME
—1 Thessalonians 3:11—4:12

An expectant hush fell over the rustic room. The director welcomed our church group to its yearly visit to Laity Lodge, a retreat center located in the hill country of Texas.

To the director's opening question, "What do you hope to find here this weekend?" we gave a myriad of answers—renewal, relaxation, fun, fellowship, and possibly, the old catfish that lives under the log! A newcomer answered, "My name is Ginny, Mary Smith's sister, from Minnesota. We have had the worst winter we have had in years. I just came here to get warm."

Ginny and I were in the same small group. We talked about living up to God's expectations. I remember saying, "It surprised me to realize that the heroes in the Old Testament stories did not always wear white hats! Sometimes, they sinned royally, and fell way short of the mark. However, they seemed to have one thing in common—remembering where home base was! Regardless of the distance they wandered, or the foreign fences they jumped, they always returned to God!"

Ginny said, "But, Carolyn, don't you think if your really worked hard at it, and urgently tried to follow Jesus' standards, that you could always remain on home base?"

"As far as I know," I replied, "Jesus Christ is the only One who did that! An elderly minister told me one time about a prayer pact that he made with a close friend. They vowed they would live out the Sermon on the Mount. When asked, 'What happened?' he replied, 'It made me sick. It was a sad day to discover that the very best I had to offer was just not good enough to be a perfect Christian. Caught up in my humanity, in the midst of this sinful world, I found my goal to be impossible.'"

In this lesson Paul is urging the Thessalonian Christians to remember Jesus' standards. He encouraged them by saying in so many words, "You can do better. More and more, you can improve your average in attempting to live His way." But Paul would be the first to admit that even with God's help, perfection will elude us.

On Sunday morning, at the close of our time together at Laity Lodge, the director asked, "Before we leave, does anyone have something he or she wants to say?" Ginny stood up and said, "I came here with my marriage in deep water, and my children in trouble. I had heard about you neat Christians at St. Matthew's, so I came down to this retreat to see how you got your act together. Then I planned to go home, clean up my kids, my marriage, and myself. After we got it all together, I would lift up the whole shiny thing to God.

"But now, my plan has changed, for I see that not even your leaders have their acts completely together! Instead, I shall return to Minnesota, offer the whole bundle, warts and all, up to God, and trust Him with the results! In the way artists fashion mosaics out of broken pieces of glass, I will trust God to do the same with me and my family."

As Ginny sat down, I thought, "You know, God, I believe Ginny got warm after all!" And as I have reflected again on Paul's thoughtful and wise words here for his Thessalonian friends, I feel warm—warm with the awarness of God's presence and determined, with His help, to "stand fast in the Lord."

LESSON 4
1 THESSALONIANS 4:13—5:5

Comfort in Death and Hope in the Lord

Lord God, Thank You for the privilege of knowing Your comfort when I feel comfortless, and Your hope when my situation seemingly has no hope. AMEN.

Most of us are very sensitive about what happens to us and to our friends at the time of death. And perhaps nothing touches our inner feelings more profoundly than a stark encounter with the reality of the grave and its relationship with the future. Two very understandable questions rise to the surface at such times: What does it mean? and What comes next?

It is questions like these that may have prompted Paul to open this part of our Scripture lesson as he did (4:13). A Thessalonian questioner may well have asked, "What about those of our Christian friends who have died?"

So often our curiosity about the future is expressed in an attempt to control not only our own lives but the lives of our survivors. Having been a lawyer before becoming a minister, I have seen all kinds of fascinating attempts to control the future by the use of wills and other testamentary dispositions. Some people have actually tried to so control and direct their estates that their holdings will con-

Death and the Future (4:13–18)
Death and Insecurity.

Attempts at Control.

tinue to accumulate wealth for three or four hundred years!

At the same time there are certain Christians who make attempts to "control the future" by a meticulous charting of future events as they are interpreted from some of the veiled or apocalyptic writings in our Bibles, such as Daniel, Ezekiel, Mark 13, the Thessalonian letters, and Revelation.

An Important Perspective.

Questions about the future are quite understandable, but an excessive preoccupation with dates and the order of events can easily cause us to lose sight of God's will for us in this world here and now. And as for dates and speculation about the signs of the end times, we are reminded of Jesus' words, "But of that day and that hour knoweth no man, no, not the angels which are in heaven, neither the Son, but the Father" (Mark 13:32). And so we have to ask, "If Jesus didn't know, how are we to know?"

Certainly, our inability as Christians to be specific about the end times is not a sign of weakness or ignorance, but rather a true awareness of the limits of human knowledge. Obviously, I believe that the coming end of the world as we know it is something we Christians need to take seriously. But I also believe that a preoccupation with charting times and events can detract us from an authentic relationship with Christ and from concern for our neighbor's welfare. To fall into that trap can easily cause us to miss the profound implications of Paul's teaching on the "last days."

The Thessalonian Question.

And so Paul responds to the question in this section of our lesson by writing, "But I would not have you to be ignorant, brethren..." (4:13). Whenever Paul used this expression, it was like a warning light being flashed, which was intended to tell his readers to pay *special* attention.

Paul flashed this signal for special attention because it had apparently been reported to him that people within the Thessalonian church were extremely concerned about their Christian friends who had died. They were evidently grieving like their pagan neighbors who were without any hope in the future.

Their confusion and sense of hopelessness seemed to center around the idea that only those who would experience the marvelous joy of meeting Christ at His Second Coming were those Christians who were alive; those who died would not share in that glory. But they were wrong, of course, and in his usual forthright manner, Paul tells them to stop grieving for their friends and loved ones as if they had no hope (4:13).

What raised doubts in their minds about their Christian friends who had died? The answer to that question has its roots in one of the crucial issues that confronts the church in any century. In this particular case, a study of early hellenistic writers and other cultural indicators of the time such as tombstones tells us that first-century people had a profound sense of hopelessness at the thought of death. Death was a bitter enemy over which there was no victory.

The Culture Drag.

So embedded was this devastating fatalism and sense of hopelessness in the face of death that the new Thessalonian Christians still reflected the mood of their Greco-Roman culture. While they had become Christians and had taken the step of faith by believing in Christ and even in His resurrection, their daily thoughts, actions, and responses had not become fully Christian. Becoming a Christian is event, process, and expectation. To *think* like a Christian takes more than simply saying yes to Jesus in an evangelistic service or in a rite of baptism. The Thessalonian Christians had taken the step of faith. They were believers (4:14), but part of their thinking—a very important part—was still quite pagan.

An awareness of this kind of cultural drag is terribly important as we encourage and nurture new Christians. How cautious we must be not to be critical and condemning of young Christians when their immaturity and "little faith" exposes flaws of unbelief. At such times we must be patient and prayerful. Throughout our studies in Paul's letters so far we have seen him as the great encourager. His tact and grace are a perpetual model for us in our Christian walk and in our relationships with new and immature believers.

It seems clear from Paul's wording here that the new Thessalonian Christians were confused about the Lord's Second Coming because they had not fully understood the meaning of Christ's resurrection and the explosive impact it was to make on their understanding of life and death. Paul wanted them to see that the resurrection was not merely the happy ending to the tragedy of Jesus' death. It was in fact the hinge point of Christianity. Without it there would be no Church, no Christianity, no New Testament,

The Significance of the Resurrection.

and we would still be slaves to sin and be without hope.

And so Paul urges his readers to let the significance of the resurrection reshape and transform their thoughts—especially thoughts about friends who had died in the Lord. They were not to mourn like people without hope, "For if we believe that Jesus died and rose again, even so them also which sleep in Jesus *will God bring with him*"(4:14, italics mine).

In discussing death Paul found in the familiar Greek euphemism of sleeping a superb picture that helped him explain the powerful nature of the resurrection. Christians who die do not, as the hellenistic writers thought, sleep with the icy permanence of cold metal. Instead, the Christian who dies in Christ will be awakened from death by the Lord's alarm clock (4:16) and will rise again. This promise is the basis for the great hope that Christians of all time have through Jesus' resurrection—the conquest of death once and for all because of that first Easter morning.

The Coming of Christ.

The coming of Christ, described here in vertical dimensions (4:16), was viewed by Paul as the central stage event of the great drama at the end of time as we know it, "For the Lord himself shall descend from heaven with a shout, with the voice of the archangel, and with the trump of God: and the dead in Christ shall rise first."

In Christ's descent—His coming from heaven—the Lord Himself will give the signal. Paul indicated that it is by the signal of His coming that the concluding events of history will be initiated. Also, other symbols are used here by Paul to describe end-events—the archangel's voice and the great trumpet of God. These are used to signal the calling of the dead in Christ to the final resurrection and the summoning of those Christians who are still alive to the great meeting with the Lord.

These apocalyptic word symbols that Paul has used here have been introduced with such force and speed that we are left almost breathless by the dynamic and powerful picture. To the first-century Christians who understood these images, the sense of encouragement must have been exceedingly strong. But to those of us accustomed to twentieth-century symbolism, the pictures may be a little confusing.

In order to understand the apocalyptic statements, wherever we find them—whether in Daniel or Revelation or here—we need to recognize that images appeal to our God-given imaginations. For example, what does Paul mean by sleeping and awaking (rising) at the coming of Christ? How does the implication of that word usage fit in with his idea as expressed in Philippians 1:23 where he speaks of departing (dying) and being with Christ?

Then, too, verses like these here in Thessalonians have led to all kinds of speculation about the state of a person after death. It has been suggested by some that dead Christians are in an in-between state which they call "soul-sleep." Others object vehemently to that idea in favor of the Christian going immediately to be with Christ.

Let's face it—our finite minds are quite incapable of understanding God's ultimate purposes and plans for the future. We don't know and don't need to know just how end-events will come together. What is important to us as we seek to live creative and full lives here and now is that the Second Coming of Christ will end the frustrations of both life and death and that as Christians our future is in God's hands. Our hope and trust is in God.

Difficulties with Apocalyptic Statements.

It will help us in comprehending this part of Paul's letter to understand that the images of "sleeping" and "rising" were used to give the new Thessalonian Christians a sense of confidence that their friends who had died would most certainly experience the wonderful day of Christ's coming whenever that would be. The purpose of the image was not to define the state, location, or nature of those who had died.

Purpose of the Sleeping Image.

While I don't believe it serves our purpose in this study to take an exhaustive look at the other images Paul used here, it may be helpful to touch on them briefly. In verse 16 reference is made to "the voice of the archangel." Actually, the concept of archangels is quite foreign to the Old Testament. But as we move through the New Testament, we find such names as Gabriel (Luke 1:19) and Michael (Jude 9 and Rev. 12:7).

The idea of archangels emerged in Jewish literature dur-

A Look at the Other Word Images.

69

ABOVE AND RIGHT. Here are two views of the Agora excavations at Thessalonica. In Paul's day this was a teeming market center for the city. Because of the Agora's seaport location, and Thessalonica as a major city on the Via Egnatia, this area was a thriving commercial center in the first century.

ing what we call the intertestamental period, approximately 300 B.C. to A.D. 50. During this time the Jews developed a view of God that pretty much removed Him directly from the concerns of humanity. It was a time when the absolute holiness of God was stressed to the point where it was believed He was not immediately involved in the affairs of humanity and acted through angels and super-angels known as archangels.

These archangels all had names ending in *el* like Michael, Gabriel, Raphael, and Uriel. *El* is the Hebrew word for God, and the archangels were supposed to act for God. They were thought to form a kind of heavenly court for God the King. This idea permeated Jewish religious thought in the first century. And so the reference in our

lesson is meant to show that it is Jesus who is in charge; He is in command. It is He and not an archangel that will announce the point of time we call the end. Our full attention must be focused on Jesus Christ, for it is in and through Him that God's will and purposes will be known.

The other image mentioned in verse 16 is "the trump of God." In the ancient world the trumpet blast was a signal by which people were called together. For the Jews, the trumpet blast was a call to worship. At the same time it was the sound of a trumpet that signaled the call to battle for ancient armies. In fact, the sound of a trumpet became a sign to the Jews of God's promised regathering of His people. So, it is understandable that this image became a symbol announcing the Second Coming of Christ, when God's people from all time would be regathered (note Isa. 27:13, Joel 2:1, and Matt. 24:31; see also the role of trumpets in Rev. 8:6–11; 15).

Some Intriguing Problems and Questions.

This part of our lesson (4:13–18) poses some interesting problems and some intriguing questions.

The first issue has to do with the expression "the word of the Lord" in verse 15. Nowhere in the Gospels do we find Jesus saying "that we which are alive and remain unto the coming of the Lord shall not prevent them which are asleep." So, it is fair to ask, "Where did Paul get this word from the Lord?"

There are two possibilities that are most likely. Either Paul got it in some mysterious way through a personal encounter with the Lord, or he may have been quoting something that had been passed on to him by others who had heard Jesus speak to this very matter. The truth is—we don't really know. But it was important for Paul's Thessalonian readers and us to know that this was not just one of Paul's ideas. He knew he had a word from the Lord on this matter.

The second intriguing issue is also found in verse 15 where Paul says "we which are alive and remain unto the coming of the Lord." Note the use of the first-person "we." What did Paul mean?

It is apparent that at this early stage of Paul's ministry and missionary activity he expected Jesus to return soon during his lifetime. In fact, Paul lived with a tremendous expectation of the coming of Christ; it made his life dynamic.

But there seemed to be a shift in Paul's mood later. When he wrote the second letter to the Corinthians, he positioned himself with those who would be dead at the time of the Lord's coming (2 Cor. 4:14). And when he wrote his letter to the Philippians from prison, we get the feeling that he was aware of his impending death.

The one thing that did not change, though, throughout all of Paul's ministry was his firm hope and expectant anticipation that the Lord *would return*. His hope and his confidence never wavered.

The third issue that captivates our thinking is found in verse 17, "...shall be caught up together..." During the last 1,900 years there have been many explanations for this and related verses. Efforts have been made to visualize this event and date it in time. It does not serve our purposes in this study, however, to become involved in a kind of "rapture" speculation and interpretation.

Important to us is the idea that the words "caught up" imply the forceful and sudden removal from this world as we know it. From Paul's perspective certain events seemed to coalesce at the Second Coming of Christ. At Christ's command the final signals would be given and those Christians who had died would be resurrected, and with the Christians who are alive, they would be "caught up" *together* to meet the Lord (4:16–17). To Paul, the how and the when were in God's hands—there was no question, though, that a triumphant meeting with Christ would take place.

Togetherness versus Separation.

The emphasis throughout these verses is on *togetherness* in contrast to the Thessalonian fear of separation—a fear that when the Lord returned, Christians who were alive would be with Christ, but those who were dead would not. Instead, Paul insisted, all Christians of all time would be united with Christ. And verse 17 concludes not merely with a statement of the togetherness of Christians but with a much more fundamental togetherness—that of Christians *with* Christ. And this is a togetherness that will never end.

Paul's Goal.

Having clearly stated his position, Paul now closed this chapter (4:18) with an instruction that summarized his discussion of the future, "Wherefore comfort one another with these words." His goal was to help his Thessalonian readers understand the power of a resurrection theology—a theology that has given Christians of all time a genuine confidence that death is not the end. Paul wanted them and us to understand that togetherness in Christ is the great hope and assurance for the Christian, and we are not to be immobilized and traumatized by the temporary separations that death brings.

Death is not to be viewed by Christians as a debilitating ultimate victor. Instead, death and separation should be seen by Christians as an interim stage in the great drama of life. The issue for each of us is to live fearlessly creative and productive lives now in anticipation of that time when there will be no more death and separation—only togetherness in Christ.

The Transition from the End to Life (5:1–5)

These opening verses of the fifth chapter of 1 Thessalonians form another transition (1–5). Paul gives us here a fascinating link between the Christian's concern for the Second Coming of Jesus and the Christian's responsibility to live an authentic life in Christ each day. Consequently these verses can apply to this lesson or the next one. But I've chosen to include them here because they give us some significant perspectives about the Second Coming of Jesus and the end of time.

The Question: When?

When Paul mentions in verse 2 "the day of the Lord," it is likely his Jewish readers especially would make the connection between his discussion here of the Second Coming of Christ and the Old Testament pictures and references to that important event. And it is understandable under the precarious circumstances in which the Thessalonian Christians lived that they would be especially interested in wanting to know *when* the Lord would come. We've seen already that they were concerned about their dead Christian friends, but they were also concerned about themselves as they went about the daily routines of life in a culture that was hostile to their Christian faith.

Paul's Response.

The fact that Jesus, as we've already seen, had said that no one would know when He would come certainly didn't keep people in the first century from speculating about His return. And so, while on one hand Paul acknowledges, "But of the times and the seasons, brethren, ye have no need that I write unto you" (5:1), he is really saying quite the opposite. He knew that emotionally they needed to be reminded, "For yourselves know perfectly that the day of the Lord so cometh as a thief in the night" (5:2). And that is precisely what he was doing.

Paul refused to become involved in a dating game, but instead he was urging the Thessalonian Christians to be prepared. But to be prepared, the apostle wanted his readers to understand that the coming day of the Lord should not be viewed as a time for a reward that God owed them. While it would be a time when faithful Christians would be united with the Lord, it would also be a time of judgment as the prophet Amos had predicted (5:18–20).

It was important to Paul for his Thessalonian readers to

so live their lives that they would not be caught off guard or unprepared irrespective as to when the Lord would come. He didn't want them to suffer a fate similar to the young women who missed the coming of the bridegroom because they weren't prepared (Matt. 25:1–13). The Christian is to be always vigilant and alert so as not to be deceived or taken by surprise.

A similar word was given to the people of the church at Sardis (Rev. 3:3). Their city was built on a seemingly impregnable mountain. In most instances they had been able to repel invading armies, but at least twice the city was captured when invaders approached it on the backside at night when unprepared guards were caught by surprise.

Paul never minimized the dangers we face as Christians. He knew the power of evil and the subtleties of temptation. He knew also that Christianity was never meant to be a comforting security blanket that promises everything will turn out all right no matter what we do. To emphasize security, safety, and complacency without obedience to the demands of the gospel is a bit like certifying a building is earthquake-safe when it is not equipped to weather a minor jolt. Outwardly such a building might appear safe, but the screams of victims after a major shock like the recent one that struck Mexico City is a stark reminder that things aren't always as they seem.

Paul and the Clock.

In this closing part of our Scripture for this lesson Paul wants his readers of all time to know without question that the Second Coming of Christ—the day of the Lord—was a sure thing even though he refused to predict the time. Further, he wanted us all to understand that for those who refused to listen to God there would be no escape from His judgment (5:3). And so the heart of this part of Paul's message at this point was that while we cannot date the coming of the Lord, we can be sure that it will be a time of judgment for those who refused the Good News of Jesus Christ. At the same time we can be certain of that coming event without knowing the specific details.

Not a Messenger of Bad News.

But there is another side to Paul's teaching here that needs to be emphasized. He was not a messenger of bad news. And his references to the day of the Lord and to judgment were not meant to be frightening.

Rather, Paul wanted his readers to discover the happy

balance between the assurance that was theirs as Christians and warning against being disobedient in their stewardship. He reminds them they "are not in darkness"—not to be taken by surprise. Rather, "Ye are all children of light, and the children of the day…" (5:5). As people living in the light of God, they should act like it in the give-and-take of their day-to-day world. And now that his word about the coming of the Lord and how his readers should view the end of time had been given, Paul shifted to the importance of living an authentic Christian life in the world.

Beyond Curiosity to Hope!

Almost 2,000 years have passed since Christ died on the cross and rose from the grave on the third day. Many generations have come and gone since Paul wrote the words we have been studying to the Christians in the church at Thessalonica. And we are still looking expectantly to the future. It is important, though, that we not be caught up in dating or trying to chart the sequence of events. Rather, we are to concentrate on living rich and full lives now.

The first-century world was a precarious place for the early Christians, and the twentieth-century world with its capacity for destruction is also frightening. Life is uncertain and brief at best. But life "in Christ" is not precarious or uncertain—it is Good News. The biblical message for the Christian—for you and me—is one of hope. The resurrected Lord has come and *He is coming again!*

Christ comes first to us in our personal lives and gives meaning to the frustrations, pains, and hurts that plague us at home, at work, and at school. And He promises to come in power at the end of time as we know it and give meaning to all of history. Our hope is fixed in this promise, and with that hope we can make sense out of anything that happens to us in the nitty-gritty of our twenty-four hour days, including every relationship of life.

Dear God, I cannot thank You enough for the meaning You've brought to my life. Your assurance is firm; my hope in You is secure and cannot be assailed. AMEN.

WHAT THIS SCRIPTURE MEANS TO ME
—1 Thessalonians 4:13—5:5

As I drove up the hospital drive, I thought, "What am I doing here? Lord, I really don't want to talk to these people!" But after refusing several invitations to speak to "Parents Forever," I finally ran out of excuses and said, "I'll come!"

This group has no long line of people desiring membership. The initiation fee is sobering: the loss of a child. Once before, I had met with a similar group, and I could still remember those sad faces mirrored in pain. The grief over the loss of a child is as old as the beginning of forever. The fear of this loss will march hand in hand into the future with all parents who dare to love.

Before finding the meeting room, I met a friend in the corridor. She was there to hear a lecture on some new theory about human behavior. That certainly wasn't my talk!

I finally found the meeting place. Seeing those hurting people flooded me with painful memories. For thirty minutes I talked about my own experiences of walking through their same darkness. Then, with a sense of urgency, they started firing questions. But above all they wanted to know what kind of future, if any, they had with their children.

The Thessalonian Christians, because they believed the Second Coming of Christ to be imminent, may have phrased their questions differently. But the bottom line was pretty much the same as the Parents Forever group, "What is going to happen to those we love? Will we ever see them again?"

Paul, in our lesson, seems to say "absolutely!" However, such questions like theirs cannot be looked up with answers verified in reference books; they can only be looked at and verified through the eyes and experience of faith:

> When death marches through
> And snatches a friend,
> Your cry bombards heaven:
> Is this really the end?
>
> You can ponder on that one
> Ten years and a day,
> But the answers elude you...
> Quit pondering and pray!

> Let prayer be your mainstay,
> A disciplined thrust.
> God's reality will brighten.
> And so will your trust.*

We really do seem to live our lives out between so many questions and elusive answers. One question from the Parents Forever group that night hit me with the force of a Texas blue norther, "What would you do if you lost another child?"

"Just thinking of that possiblity paralyzes me with fear." I responded. "Some of our friends have lost two children. When I first heard of their second tragedy, I felt fear for me, instead of pain for them. If it could happen to them again, why not me?"

"This thought scared me to death! In thinking of our agonizing feeling of loss when little Carl died, I feel certain that I could never survive such a devastating blow. Surely, this time I would sink into the mire and quicksand, never to be seen again. But then I have to admit that I don't recall God's ever promising me strength for tomorrow or for those future 'what if' days. He only promises me strength and His presence in my 'now' moments." The ancient writer said it well, "And as thy days, so shall thy strength be " (Deut. 33:25).

Paul kept reminding those early Christians that Jesus was their hope. And I really believe that! He has been absolutely loving and faithful in my past. Can I trust Him to be the same in my fragile future? And, on my better days, I can say "yes!"

*Carolyn Huffman. *Life Between The Questions*. Word Publishing, Waco. 1985. pp.36f.

LESSON 5
1 THESSALONIANS 5:6–28

Living as Children of Light

Dear Savior, Let my life reflect Your light, Your love, Your joy, Your spontaneity and enthusiasm, Your love for righteousness and judgment, Your compassion, Your peace. AMEN.

Unfortunately, at various times throughout the history of the church there have been divided opinions as to the relationship of Christian belief or doctrine to Christian action. This break between believing and living, as we discussed in Lesson 3, is entirely foreign to Paul's writings and to the entire New Testament.

The Social Gospel emphasis that was present in part of the church in the early twentieth century was an attempt to put a heart into Christian life and preaching. In some instances, though, the social concern was not accompanied by a sound basis in belief. And as a result of the controversies that raged then, there continues to be a question in the minds of many believers about Christian social responsibilities.

Because of this confusion Christians are often polarized into two "goody" groups—the "do-goodies" and the "believe-goodies." As so often happens, many in these two groups tend to feel they have a corner on the truth. But throughout all of Paul's writings the point is clearly made that our Christian beliefs are not something apart from the

Basic Perspectives in Living for Christ (5:6–11)

Personal Behavior and Social Concern.

way we live and relate to people around us—belief and action are inseparable.

But in spite of the New Testament emphasis on both belief and action the feeling seems to persist in many places that society today is far too complicated and so hopelessly evil that there really is nothing we as Christians can do about it. Persons who believe that way concentrate their efforts on personal morals and salvation and ignore Christian responsibility to rectify the wrongs that persist in our society.

It was great and noble Christians like William Wilberforce and Lord Shaftsbury in nineteenth-century England who worked relentlessly to improve the intolerable working conditions of young children and poor people in the factories. The major reforms in English labor laws came about because of Christian concern for people.

Again and again, it has been Christian influences that founded hospitals and related places of healing for the care and relief of suffering. And it has been those same influences, in the United States at least, that founded many of the major universities—places of learning that have elevated the welfare of people and raised society's standards.

The correcting of sweatshop conditions, the enacting of humane labor laws, a passionate concern for the poor and hungry in our world, involvement in efforts to correct the evils that promote terrorism and war—all of these, and more, are the concern of the Christian who loves God and neighbor.

Some Christians take the position that Paul had little concern for changing society in his day because he didn't personally attack slavery. But while he didn't have the power to free the slaves, his attitude on slavery seems clearly reflected as he charged Philemon of Colossae to treat Onesimus like a brother and not a slave (Philm. 15–18). And then as the centuries rolled by, we see that it was Paul's words and attitudes that eventually formed the foundation for the great moral and spiritual revolutions that have elevated people and instigated change for better in society.

As Christians, we must never shrug our shoulders listlessly in the face of human need, wherever we find it. We are never to feel that reform efforts are futile. But also as Christians, we are realists. It is true that sin and evil and unfairness are a part of our present world, but as agents of Jesus Christ, we are to confront those forces and work for change in His name.

Paul's Perspective.

It seems perfectly clear from the way Paul wrote in this letter that he believed it was imperative for Christians to act out their faith in daily life and practice if non-Christians were to be influenced by the Good News. In the last lesson we looked closely at Paul's words and feelings about the end of time as we know it. On the surface it might appear that this discussion centered entirely around theology and doctrine. Not so! For it was at this point that he focused on giving advice to his readers on how to live authentic Christian lives.

Paul's advice here was deadly serious and of major importance because of their crippling misconception about the Second Coming of Christ. They had apparently become lazy Christians who were completely unconcerned about surrounding conditions and their personal responsibilities. The only thing that seemed to matter to them was Jesus' soon coming. The apostle's response to this faulty way of thinking closed out our last lesson, "Ye are all the children of light, and the children of the day: we are not of the night, nor of darkness" (5:5). And immediately following comes the opening verse of our Scripture for this lesson, "Therefore let us not sleep, as do others; but let us watch and be sober" (5:6).

In line with his usual custom in writing, Paul's "therefore" points to what he has written before and says in effect—because of that, do this. He is telling his Thessalonian readers here that with a proper understanding of the Second Coming of Christ their lives as Christians are to be different. As "children of light," the symbol of good, they do not belong to the night, the symbol of evil. And so he reminds them they are to be alive, alert, watchful. They are not to be asleep or sluggish or drunk, but wide awake and sober.

Watchfulness.

The mood of these verses (5:5–8) pulsates with the same watchfulness theme that is found in a number of Jesus' teachings. For example, in His story of the householder in Matthew 24:43 and in the story of the ten virgins in Matthew 25:1–12 the emphasis is on "Watch" or "Be alert."

The point Paul wants to get across here, though, with

his emphasis on watchfulness is not entirely related to the Second Coming and the end of time on earth. Rather, it is on how an "end time" perspective should affect the daily life of the Christian in the present. And to bring it even closer to home in the twentieth century, how are we who also have a hope in the future to live in our own particular worlds in the face of the demands that family, home, vocation, and social obligation make upon us? It is important that we be continually reminded of the truth that our Christianity is not merely a "by and by" proposition; it is here and now.

Christian Preparation.

Paul then points out to his Thessalonian readers that in addition to being alert and sober they are to put "on the breastplate of faith and love; and for an helmet, the hope of salvation" (5:8). Once again Paul refers to familiar Old Testament images (Isa. 59:17) and applies them to the Christian walk. We saw this idea greatly amplified, as you will remember in the stirring metaphor Paul used in his letter to the Christians at Ephesus, in which his description of a soldier's armament helped to illustrate our spiritual battle.

You will remember how Christian was armed in his fight with a devil-like figure called Apollyon in John Bunyan's *Pilgrim's Progress*. It coincided exactly with Paul's description in Ephesians of how a believer is to be dressed and armed as a soldier for the Lord. But the intriguing thing about the armor Christian wore in *Pilgrim's Progress* was that there was no protection for his back—he dare not turn and run. This gives us a vivid picture of how Christians are to confront life head-on with no thought of retreat. We dare not turn our backs on the forces of evil.

Soldier and Servant.

For Paul, retreat was an unthinkable option in his service for the Lord, and this attitude was clearly seen throughout all of his missionary career. It is quite likely this strong feeling had its beginnings at the time of his first visit to Thessalonica. You will recall in our study of Acts 15 that Paul was forced out of both Thessalonica and Berea where those opposed to the gospel he and Silas were preaching stirred up a threatening mob scene.

Paul knew then that his real enemy in his battle for the hearts of people was Satan himself (1 Thess. 2:18). So we don't have to stretch our imaginations very far to see that Paul felt the soldier image—like the servant image (Rom.

1:1)—symbolized his own life as a Christian. At the same time it is apparent in all of Paul's writings that he believed this same servant-soldier image should characterize the life of any faithful follower of Jesus Christ. The servant image clearly represents the Christian's relationship with God. And the soldier image fits the Christian's conflict with the forces of evil.

Unfortunately, at times the soldier image tends to become a bit confused and blurred, at least as it relates to who Christians may think the real enemy is. I'm sure we've all been aware that there are those who talk and act as if other Christians were the enemy—those whose worship and understanding of the faith differ from our own interpretations and patterns. But our attacks, as followers of the Lord Jesus, are to be directed against the forces of evil, the powers of darkness, and *not* against our fellow believers. It is to these forces that we are to be alert, while at the same time we are to live in unity with other Christians as Paul so often emphasized.

A Defensive Posture.

You will remember from earlier studies that both the breastplate and helmet are primarily defensive pieces of armor. These images fit in very closely with the defensive posture that we find throughout 1 Thessalonians. This letter as a whole carries a strong note of encouragement because Paul knew his readers faced severe difficulties in their Christian pilgrimage. This encouragement theme surfaces again just a few words beyond the armor images in verse 11, "Wherefore comfort yourselves together, and edify one another..."

In all of Paul's writings he never minimized the difficulties or the temptations that confront Christians. At the same time, though, he was always the great encourager. In this, Paul models for us a pattern that is essential in our relationship with our brothers and sisters in Christ. We change and grow through expressions of love and affirmation—criticism is destructive; encouragement is always constructive.

The Christian Graces and Salvation.

We see in these verses that in speaking of encouragement to his readers Paul linked the picture of armor with his famous triad of Christian graces, which he introduced at the very beginning of the letter and which we discussed in Lesson 1. And the order here is the same—faith, love, and hope. As I mentioned in Lesson 1, the order Paul gives these graces here can quite easily be linked to the three stages of salvation. But in this reference, by separating hope from faith and love, it becomes linked *directly* with salvation. In other words, the point Paul seems to be making here is that hope—the last stage in the salvation process—should definitely make a difference in the "here-and-now lives" of the Thessalonian believers.

This same truth applies to Christians of all time—our future hope will have a marked effect on the way we live today. If we have little or no hope and expectations for the future, we are likely to be careless and indifferent about the way we live in the present. But if living *with* God is a genuine "beyond-this-life" goal for us, we will believe and live now in a way that fulfills His purposes for us. This is precisely why as Christians living in a late twentieth-century world we are to be as alert and sober as Paul urges his first-century readers to be (5:8).

The Death of Jesus and Its Significance.

As Paul moves now toward the conclusion of this assurance and encouragement section, he reminds his readers that it isn't God's intention to condemn us—"For God hath not appointed us to wrath" or judgment, but rather that we might "obtain salvation by our Lord Jesus Christ, who died for us..." (5:9–10). This is the grand Good News of the gospel, *Jesus took our place!*

Paul also wants us to see that Jesus' death on the cross should make a revolutionary difference in the way we Christians look at ourselves. As we reflect on all that God has done for us in Christ, we begin to understand the incredible fact that *God really does care about us.* Our acceptance of this awesome truth gives us an entirely different perspective on ourselves and on the way we live and the priorities we set for ourselves.

Alive with Christ.

The words of encouragement move to a climax in the latter part of verse 10 as Paul speaks to their first great question, "Whether we wake or sleep, we should live together with him." In other words, whether Christians have died by the time of Jesus' Second Coming or are still alive, we are assured that we will all be united and will "live together with him" (5:10).

The Greek word "live," which Paul used here introduces a new stage of life—a time when Christians from all centuries will be joined together in the great experience of the resurrection and live forever with the Lord. This expectation is the Christian's encouragement and hope. It is the grand motivation to live Godly lives here and now.

A later writer, as he looked far into the future, expressed that new stage of life as being a time when "he will dwell with them, and they shall be his people, and God himself shall be with them, and be their God. And God shall wipe away all tears from their eyes; and there shall be no more death, neither sorrow, nor crying, neither shall there be any more pain..." (Rev. 21:3–4).

And so, in effect, Paul is saying in verse 11 to the Thessalonian Christians and to us—because of this great hope you have both for now and the future, *encourage and comfort and build up each other*.

Having concluded his comments on how Christians should live in anticipation of Christ's Second Coming, Paul now gives us some brief instructions on Christian attitudes and actions. The tone here is quite similar to the pithy instructions found in Romans 12.

Instructions in Outline (5:12–22)

Paul's first set of instructions to the Thessalonian Christians have to do with their attitude toward their church leaders (5:12–13). First, they are to recognize (know) them, verse 12, and respect them, verse 13.

The basis for acknowledging leadership at this stage of the early church was evidently not determined by either election or appointment. Rather, it was apparently based on a recognition of those who were faithfully serving in leadership roles. In other words, as people worked together in the congregation, certain qualities of leadership seemed to emerge. And when leaders became apparent, the rest were urged to acknowledge and respect them. Then, as now, I'm sure a willingness to serve was an important prerequisite.

Attitudes Toward Leaders.

From Paul's wording in these verses, especially in the Greek, there were three important functions or attributes of a leader. First, worthy leaders are viewed as those who are diligent and active in the Christian community. But the implication is even more forceful than that—leaders of the church are to be committed to the sacrificial giving of themselves, rather than getting for themselves. Leaders

Attributes of a Leader.

85

are not to jockey for position or to be power grabbers.

Second, leaders are to be devoted to a caring ministry of service. Given the context of verse 12, and the general emphasis of Paul in all of his writings on service rather than status, it seems likely that the words "over you" inadequately express the original meaning.

While leadership in the church does require a certain amount of management, it can better be understood in terms of caring and shepherding service. As a Servant-Leader, Jesus gave us the prime model for leadership, and most certainly this was the style Paul introduced into the early church. Authoritarian models may be efficient, but the spirit of servant leadership can easily be lost. The domineering temptation in leadership is an ever-present threat to all church congregations, and this weakness was forcefully confronted in the New Testament.

Stop just a moment and read 1 Peter 5:2–4 in your Bible. Here is pictured the supreme alternative to power-grabbing leadership—loving and caring service, self-giving. Interesting enough, this is a model just now being introduced into the business world. To many, this is a new idea. But to the Christian, it is the pattern of leadership given to us by Jesus and Paul.

The third aspect of leadership that we find in verse 12 involves instruction or warning, "admonish you." Paul was extremely sensitive of the need the early Christians had for teaching and instruction. He was quite sure that as the gospel moved into new settings there would be new challenges confronting the Christians—new and important issues to be faced. This would require able leadership that is adequately prepared to give instruction. Able leadership in interpreting God's work and the ability to apply it to the varying settings of life is a critical need in every church.

Respect for Leaders.

Paul next moves on to urge his readers to show a proper respect for their leaders, not because of their status or power but because of the servant work they were doing (5:13). Respectful recognition is due those who are actively serving the Lord in positions of leadership.

The Mark of Leadership.

We don't know precisely what prompted Paul's closing words in verse 13, "And be at peace among yourselves," but there can be no doubt as to the importance of this admonition. Christians are to be people of peace as followers of the Prince of Peace. But unfortunately our witness becomes smeared all too often by conflict among Christians and within the church. Certainly, Paul's urging to his first-century friends in Thessalonica is very appropriate for our day, "Be at peace among yourselves."

Paul next turns his attention to four particular concerns among the weak members of the Christian community (5:14). He first identifies the "unruly." Lazy and disorderly Christians are warned to correct their errant life-styles.

Second, Paul urges those who are fainthearted, discouraged, or frightened to be encouraged. Those who are fearful and apprehensive about the future need to be given assurance and comfort. The King James translation "feeble-

Paul's Instructions to Faltering Christians.

A general view of the Macedonian countryside as we see it today. It is a fertile area with a mountainous interior.

minded" is much too strong. Instead, the important message here is that the fainthearted and those with low self-esteem are to be encouraged to feel good about themselves, to have the assurance they are worthwhile and that they count.

Third, those who are spiritually weak in the faith are to be given a helping hand. So often within the Christian community we see the tendency to reject those who are weak and somehow don't quite measure up. But Paul is urging his readers to be supportive of those who are struggling and having a hard time making it.

Fourth, Paul urges that we "be patient toward all." The Greek word he used here speaks of being patient with people. This quality of patience is one that Paul stresses; he sees it as the result of the Holy Spirit at work in the life of the Christian (see also Gal. 5:22).

These four exhortations or urgings of Paul give us a marvelous picture of the concern we Christians are to have for our brothers and sisters in the Lord. We find nothing judgmental in Paul's attitude here. Instead, we are urged to build up and be supportive of our fellow members of the Body of Christ.

A Christian Perspective.

Now, Paul's concerns expressed in these four exhortations seemed to spark his need to set down a generalized warning, "See that none render evil for evil unto any man; but ever follow that which is good, both among yourselves, and to all men" (5:15). The "eye for an eye" or law of revenge theme (see Ex. 21:24 and Lev. 24:20) in which pity was rejected (see Deut. 19:21) had been the accepted pattern in the early period of Israel's existence. Jesus firmly rejected the "eye for an eye" concept and replaced it by turning the other cheek and loving one's enemy (see Matthew 5:38–48).

Furthermore, for Paul, who was a disciple of the open-minded Gamaliel (Acts 22:3), and the more liberal Hillel tradition—the way of Christian love meant an even more radical perspective. Not only did Paul affirm the so-called negative golden rule found in Judaism—"to not do to others what you would not want done to you"—he urged the early Christians not to repay evil for evil (1 Thess. 5:15 and Rom. 12:17). He also staunchly advocated Jesus' positive perspective of doing good to each other and to all people (1 Thess. 5:15 and Gal. 6:10; see also Matt. 7:12).

From these teachings we see that to follow in the footsteps of Jesus and Paul in our Christian pilgrimage doesn't mean merely to avoid doing bad things to other people. Rather, it means seeking aggressively the opportunity to help others in need, whatever those needs may be.

Paul now continues with a second group of brief but very important instructions (5:16–18). The emphasis of these is upon attitudes that are characteristic of a mature Christian way of living—1) Be joyful and happy under all conditions; 2) Pray continually; and 3) Be thankful for everything.

Instructions on Spiritual Living.

Be joyful and happy under all conditions. Unfortunately, genuine joy is all too often a missing element in the lives of many Christians. But it is most certainly an attitude that marks people who are really alive in Jesus Christ. It is important, though, for us to understand that the joyful attitude Paul is commanding his readers to have is far more than a surface happiness we feel when all is going well and we are getting our way.

For the Christian, joy is not to be some isolated experience but a perpetual way of life. With a deeply rooted faith and trust in Jesus Christ we can feel a reassuring inner joy even during our hard times—those moments that from a human point of view seem hopeless. The Christian is to "rejoice evermore," during periods of testing, when things aren't going the way we want them to go, during those times when we feel alone, through hours of illness and bereavement—always and under all conditions.

Pray continually. Paul's second instruction-command is that for the Christian, prayer is a continuous activity. Now, when the apostle said this, he knew we can hardly be on our knees all the time. And, obviously, he wasn't pointing us to a complete life of quiet and solitude.

For Paul, prayer was more than a matter of words and body posture. It was a way of life that involved a constant awareness of the presence of God. There is a vast difference between *saying* prayers and *being prayerful*. Being prayerful includes when we're shopping for groceries, wrestling with a problem in the office, enjoying a television program.

Praying continually is more than rushing to God when we're in trouble or facing a crisis. It is more than a desperate cry for help when a child is sick or when money runs low or when we lose a loved one. Praying continually is living in an attitude of prayer even when we're involved in the routines and nitty-gritty details of daily life.

In addition, I believe, this instruction-command involves certain definite disciplines. For example, regular and planned Bible reading accompanied by purposeful prayer and reflection is essential to living all day in an attitude of prayer. Each person can adapt these times to his or her daily rhythms.

Centuries ago Clement of Alexandria worded it simply when he said, "Prayer is conversation with God"—pray continually.

Be thankful for everything. Paul's third instruction-command appears to be virtually impossible. However, we learn from the apostle here and in other places that an attitude of gratitude should be the norm for the Christian in the midst of all circumstances.

From Paul's perspective, "thanksgiving" was not to be confined to one day of the year. But unfortunately, even our national Thanksgiving Day in November is so devoted to turkey and dressing and football that it is likely too many people completely forget to be thankful to God.

Somehow, though, thankfulness—this attitude of gratitude—needs to become a greater part of our lives. But this can only happen as we remember daily that we have been blessed with God's great gift—His Son. It can happen, too, as we remember that God is at work in this world of ours. It was this truth that enabled Paul to write in another place: *we know that in all things God works together for good to them that love God, to them who are the called according to his purpose* (Rom. 8:28).

Thanking God daily for the great gift of His Son and for every event and person that touches our lives is a transforming experience. And with the passing of time, even for those things that seemed bad to us and for which it was hard to be thankful, we will come to see that in God's eternal purpose, they were good."

Christian Life and the Will of God.

Paul then goes on to write that when we are joyful, when we pray, and when we are thankful, we are in "the will of God in Christ Jesus" (5:18)—we are God-centered people and not self-centered. As Christians, we come to see that everything that happens in life of lasting value comes from God. Is it any wonder then that Paul concluded this part of our lesson with the assurance that if we live by these instruction-commands, we will be in the will of God?

Instructions on Spiritual Issues.

The final group of instructions that Paul had for his Thessalonian readers and us relate directly to certain spiritual issues that confront Christians and the church (5:19–22). First, he urges them to "Quench not the Spirit." It is quite likely that in Thessalonica, as in Corinth, there were those who had gone overboard in the way they expressed the gifts of the Spirit. It was the misuse of spiritual gifts that caused some Christians to reject them entirely.

You will recall our study of the excesses that existed within the church at Corinth. It was these that caused Paul to set down the guidelines found in 1 Corinthians 12, 13, and 14. And it may have been a similar problem that caused him to caution the Thessalonian Christians here. And Paul's word is a very appropriate warning for us in our church life today. We are to avoid all forms of overreaction so as not to suppress the work of God's Spirit in our lives and in the world.

Next then, Paul writes, "Despise not prophesyings." While we are not exactly sure what form this gift of prophesying took in Thessalonica, it is apparent that whatever it was, it must have created some negative reactions.

The best definition we have of the gift of prophesy was a part of our studies in 1 Corinthians 14 where Paul wrote, "But he that prophesieth speaketh unto men to edification, and exhortation, and comfort" (verse 3). In other words, the reference here is apparently to those from within the congregation who felt they had a word from the Lord. And so Paul is advising his friends to be attentive to that word (5:20).

Paul now closes this set of instructions with two sound words of advice for Christians of all time (5:21–22). No matter what questions and issues arise within the church, we are to first examine and test them ("Prove all things"), and second, we are to avoid "all appearance of evil." Our standard for testing and proving what is right, however, must always be the Scriptures, the Word of God.

The Climactic Prayer and Conclusion (5:23–28)

Paul brought this entire instructional section to a climax with a sensitive prayer—one of his most beautiful benedictions—that his Thessalonian friends may continue in the salvation process (5:23–24).

A Prayer of Assurance.

In verse 23 Paul prays that his readers may give themselves wholly to God and as whole persons they might be fully prepared and without blame at the Second Coming of Christ. This was not a call to any form of superficial piety. Rather it was a call for them and it is a call for us to holy living under the guidance and with the power of the Holy Spirit.

And to that prayer Paul adds the assurance that God is trustworthy and reliable (5:24). He doesn't abandon us in the process of living but sees us through in our pilgrimage to holiness.

The great Good News that Paul has for us here is that *God is with us!* We need never think of ourselves as Lone Rangers. God is our helper, supporter, and guide. This is our assurance under every circumstance of life.

A Prayer Request.

Paul's request, "Pray for us" was deadly serious. There was nothing casual about these words. Paul knew that he and his missionary associates were absolutely dependent on God working through them and that they desperately needed the prayer support of their friends and fellow Christians.

There is perhaps nothing more assuring to us than to know that loved ones and friends are praying for us. And one of our greatest privileges as Christians comes as we pray specifically for the needs of others. E. M. Bounds, noble Christian and writer, worded it this way, "Talking to men for God is a great thing, but talking to God for men is greater still."

Paul Ends the Letter.

In verse 26 Paul asks his readers to greet all his Christian friends in Thessalonica with a "holy kiss" (5:26). This was a common form of greeting in the early church that conveyed a sense of the community at peace and in harmony with each other. This custom is still a part of some eastern cultures. In ours, hugging or a handshake is more common. But by this greeting Paul wanted his friends to be reminded of his deep love and concern for them.

It is this sense of caring and of community that so needs to be revived in our church today in America. With our spread out and mobile society we have lost much of that Christian intimacy that characterized the church during its strongest and most vital periods.

And then for a moment the tone seems to change as Paul issues a strong word of command in which he charges his immediate readers to see to it that the letter is read publicly to all of the Christians in Thessalonica. There was no doubt in Paul's mind as to the importance of this letter. He saw this as a powerful and authoritative word to all of the Christians at Thessalonica. He had opened up his heart to them as their apostle-pastor. His message was clear: The Lord is coming! Live like He *is* coming!

And with that, Paul gives his beloved friends a final benediction—a suitable ending to a gracious and loving letter: "The grace of our Lord Jesus Christ be with you. Amen."

Everlasting Father, Let the revival of Christian intimacy begin with me. Help me to truly care about others with the caring and love of Christ. AMEN.

WHAT THIS SCRIPTURE MEANS TO ME
—1 Thessalonians 5:6–28

On sabbatical leave in 1980 Chuck and I studied at St. George's Anglican College in Jerusalem. It was a fascinating course taken with other Christians from all over the world.

One day, hot, tired, and covered with dust from walking the ancient streets of the Old City, we straggled in for our afternoon tea break. Sam, an Australian classmate, carefully balancing his cup, walked over and joined us. "Carolyn," he said, "I know a little about handwriting analysis. Write me some sentences on this card, and let me tell you about yourself."

After examining my writing, Sam said quietly, "Carolyn, you may have been creative at one time in your life, for I understand you published a book, but in this present moment, I see no creativity at all."

I didn't know anything about Sam's ability as a handwriting analyst, but he certainly nailed me with a painful truth. In the frantic pace of exploring, studying, and seeing so many of the historical landmarks of God's story, I had forgotten to stay in touch with the Architect, Himself.

Actually, months before my trip, I had neglected to carve out some priority time to be alone with God, and had cut myself off from the Source of all creation. Every time I do this I shortchange myself, and I shortchange God.

In verse twelve of our lesson Paul lists some important behavior models for the Thessalonian Christians. By verse fourteen the message changes from simple requesting to an imperative urging.

By the time Paul reaches verse seventeen, he unequivocally declares to the Thessalonians, "Pray without ceasing." Toward the end of the letter, Paul assures them of his own prayer support, and says, "Brethren, pray for us." Without a doubt, prayer was essential to Paul.

For years I ran away from the distasteful word "discipline." I wanted to be a balanced, mature, insightful Christian, but I wanted to get there by just "going about." I soon discovered, however, that every mature Christian whom I had met or read about seemed to have one thing in common: daily time to pray and be alone with God. Each person who really seemed to have a firm grip on life gave priority to that very special time.

This quality prayer time makes a difference to me, too. On the days that I remember to start my morning with prayer, I seem to be able to handle life better. Life is not necessarily free from storms, but I seem to steer more adroitly through the rough waters. Unfortunately, I don't always remember to do this.

A simple prayer that has been a lifeline to me is one my mother taught me. She once said, "Carolyn, there is great power and healing in the words, 'Lord, Thou knowest.'" Saying this prayer over and over again in the crisis times of my life when I have been in a spiritual desert, in emotional overload, or mental doubt and confusion has brought me great peace. It keeps me in constant contact with the One who holds all the answers and is always faithful.

Paul pleads with his Thessalonian friends to live by certain standards. For me, the only way I can come close to doing these difficult things is to try to pray without ceasing. Prayer always makes a difference!

LESSON 6
2 THESSALONIANS 1:1–12

A Suffering Church

Almighty God, Help me to hear Your voice above all the voices and distractions in my life. AMEN.

Sometimes it is easy for us who live with the concerns and frustrations of the twentieth century to idealize the early church or to think about the early Christians as perfect models of obedience and understanding. A brief reading of Paul's Corinthian letters reveals that early Christians were subject to all kinds of temptations—including sexual immorality, legal battles, struggles over proper worship patterns, and crucial differences of viewpoint on doctrinal matters. In this respect their problems were first-century replicas of those which we experience today.

But it is even more important for us to see how the early Christians responded to correction and criticism. That it was necessary for Paul to write more than one letter not only to the pesky Corinthian church but also to the church at Thessalonica is an excellent example of how hard it is for Christians to accept or fully understand correction. The tendency for most of us is to pay attention only to those things we want to hear and give little attention to what we do not wish to hear. Because of this widespread human weakness we miss so much of what the Lord wants for us.

A Second Letter (1:1–2)
*A Rationale for
2 Thessalonians.*

Undoubtedly, word had reached Paul and his missionary associates, Timothy and Silas, that their first letter hadn't corrected the wrong ideas that had permeated the church in Thessalonica, and the stage was set for this second letter. In it Paul continues to work at clearing up the false ideas about the Second Coming of Jesus and their effect on the lives of the Thessalonian Christians.

And while this letter was probably written not too long after the first one, the persecution of the Thessalonian Christians had apparently intensified. It was this and the failure to correct earlier problems in the church that made this second letter necessary.

The Salutation.

The salutation in this letter (1:1–2) is largely a repetition of the one found in 1 Thessalonians. The major difference is the double appearance this time of "God our Father" and "the Lord Jesus Christ." This double emphasis seems to strengthen, in Paul's mind, the link between Jesus and God, as well as emphasizing that God is indeed the Father of all believers. He is "our Father."

It is interesting, too, that this double emphasis involving God and Jesus became a part of most of Paul's letters. In fact, this form is found in all of them with the exception of Colossians. During this early stage of Paul's ministry he was apparently working out his pattern for expressing his thoughts about Christ.

For those of us who follow along over 1,900 years later, this linkage of Jesus with God may not seem to be an issue in our faith. But for those early first-century Christians, this identification needed to be firmly established. In this way, Paul became a model for other early Christian thinkers. For example, this same literary formula is employed in 2 Peter, and it is clear that the inspired writer there was familiar with Paul's letters (2 Pet. 3:15–16).

An Opening Thanksgiving (1:3–4)
An Intriguing Sentence.

Following the salutation, Paul launches immediately into one long and complex sentence (1:3–10). It is as though he had something so important to say that he didn't want to pause even for a moment before getting it all out. It takes a very skilled and thoughtful writer to write clear long sentences, and Paul was certainly such a person. The thought line in this sentence is both extremely important and brilliant. Let's look first at the opening phrases of the sentence.

Paul mentions first his continued feeling of gratitude for their faithfulness (1:3) even in the midst of the growing difficulties and hard times they are facing for their faith (1:4). But in looking at Paul's comments here, some interpreters sense a change of mood and tone as compared to his remarks in the first letter. Here his tone seems to be a bit more formal. Even as he congratulates his Thessalonian friends for their faithfulness, he writes with a sense of "oughtness" or "boundness" in his affirmation.

This subtle shift in tone seems a bit strange when we realize that he is writing to the very same people to whom he addressed his first letter. These are his "brethren"—his children in the faith. He is still thankful, he writes, for their faith. But, we do well to ask, "What has happened between the two letters?"

We don't know for certain, of course, but it is highly possible that enough had happened since Paul first set foot in Europe, in terms of opposition to the Christian message, to cause him to feel more keenly the imminent threat of that opposition to the Thessalonian Christians. He knew from his own experience just how difficult it was for Christians to stand firm in their faith in the midst of trouble and persecution. This had to be a most sobering experience for Paul as he realized the severity of the testing that confronted his spiritual children.

Paul's experience of feeling the pain and hardship his spiritual children in Thessalonica were enduring was very much like that of a parent who suffers when his or her natural children are going through emotional or physical difficulties and hardship. As any parent knows, it is easier to endure one's own pain than to stand helplessly by and watch a child who is sick and hurting. Somehow, as Paul speaks of the "persecutions and tribulations that ye endure," we suddenly find ourselves exposed to the raw edges of his feelings, and we, too are sobered by what must have been a most painful time for his readers.

Paul's sensitivity to the pain his Christian friends were going through gives us a model for our times. Christians in the Middle East and many Third World countries are, even while we're reading this, suffering intense physical

Gratitude and Persecution.

The Role of Trauma.

and emotional pain. Frequently, our television screens carry pictures of suffering and death in parts of our world that put us right alongside those dying from hunger or the ravages of war. We, like the Apostle Paul in his day, must not rest easy or "conduct business as usual" as long as our brothers and sisters in Christ are experiencing hardship, pain, and even death.

Christian Virtues Revisited.

Even though Paul's first letter had not corrected the problems in the Thessalonian church he continues to affirm them for their faith, love, and hope (1:3–4 and 1 Thess. 1:3). This time, however, in speaking of their faith he uses a Greek expression which means "growing magnificently," "...your faith groweth exceedingly." This is a powerful expression that appears just once in all of Paul's writings.

At the same time Paul acknowledges that their love for one another is "increasing" or "developing in abundance." And while hope is not directly mentioned here, we can tell from the tone of this long and complex sentence that Paul is writing to encourage his readers to have even more hope.

The apostle wanted his readers to understand that these three Christian characteristics or virtues are what sets the believer in Christ apart from everyone else. There's nothing static about faith in Christ. It is dynamic, living and growing—as is our love for one another. And it is because of that faith and love that we have an eternal hope—not based on external conditions at any given period of time. Rather, these virtues become a way of life for the Christian because of the internal confidence we have in God.

There is a powerful twentieth-century lesson in this first-century setting. Paul wasn't writing with religious language in a pious framework. He in Corinth and his friends in Thessalonica were living in a real and at times raw world. For them life was difficult and complex. Easy and flip answers were no more satisfying for them than they are for us.

As we have discovered in our studies so far, there was nothing naive or simplistic about Paul. It is obvious that his education in both Tarsus and Jerusalem was of the finest. It is equally obvious that he understood the thinking and culture of his Greek world. And yet we see him in both of these letters encouraging and affirming the Christians in Thessalonica for living on a day-to-day basis with faith in

God and love for one another. And while much has changed in the interval between the first century and the twentieth, nothing in the expansion of human knowledge and understanding has taken the place of these virtues in creative and wholesome human relationships. Paul was very up-to-date in his thinking and understanding.

Growing Toward Maturity.

We also catch another important thought as we look carefully at Paul's words in verse 3 as he emphasizes the *growth* of the Thessalonian Christians. It was not enough to merely *possess* faith and love, the Christian is to *grow* in the understanding and practice of these virtues. Growth is an important movement in the maturing process of authentic believers in Jesus Christ. In other words, there is no status quo for the Christian; there is nothing static about our faith. Either we grow or we lose ground.

Even though the Thessalonian Christians were having faith problems in other areas, they obviously measured up to Paul's expectations by their growth in faith and love. This we see in Paul's comment, "...we ourselves glory in you" (1:4); "we ourselves boast about you." As their spiritual father, Paul was justly proud of them. And as is common in other of his letters, he never hesitated to be affirmative and encouraging when he could. And Paul is certainly a model of a proud parent; he was never blind to problems or the presence of evil, but he was always the affirmer and encourager of those who sought to grow in Christ.

A Model of Consistency.

Paul's model of being a spiritual parent and mentor to the Thessalonian Christians was ideal simply because he himself had modeled the self-sacrificing spirit of Christ during his times of hardship and persecution. They obviously understood his example well because they copied him even as he copied Christ (see the concept of modeling and imitation in 2 Cor. 8:1–7 and Phil. 3:17).

We've all heard the saying, I'm sure, that an idea or an example is better caught than taught. Watching and listening to an authentic living example is far more powerful than listening to an ineffective or inconsistent spokesman for God. By their actions the Thessalonian Christians were duplicating the spirit of Paul.

The application of this modeling example is still meant

to be a vital part of our Christian walk. Each of us is called to be a mentor—an example—to our families, friends, fellow church members, and to people in the marketplace and crossroads of life. It is sobering to realize that people are watching us and may well be modeling their lives after what they see in us. Our challenge is to encourage others even as Paul by his life and example encouraged the Christians in Thessalonica.

A Further Message of Encouragement (1:5–10)
A Poetic Message.

Having expressed his gratitude for his readers' faithfulness in the opening words of this letter, Paul now goes on to assure the Thessalonian Christians that God would reward them for their faithfulness.

Anyone familiar with ancient poetry and hymnody may recognize the poetical nature of verses 6 through 10. Verse 5 seems to serve as an introduction to this poetical segment. We can't be sure here whether Paul was using some form of an existing hymn or was actually waxing poetic himself as he attempted to encourage his readers' continued faithfulness by referring to that future time when God will take "vengeance on them that know not God, and that obey not the gospel of our Lord Jesus Christ" (1:8). At that same time, he reminds them they will be rewarded for their faithfulness.

A Twofold Sign.

As Paul continued to lay out the truth he wanted his readers to get, he indicates that their faithfulness and endurance in the midst of difficult times were in reality powerful signs of God's righteous judgment in the affairs of the human race. He acknowledges that their faithfulness in not giving in to the forces of evil was a most significant witness—both to Christians and non-Christians. It was true, or course, that each would be judged differently, and then Paul moves on to spell out the implications to both.

A Sign for Christians.

To Christians in the Roman world of the first century, the faithfulness of the Thessalonian believers was an indication of God's guiding and superintendent presence with them. For Paul, the righteous judgment of God was never merely a negative idea. It had a positive side as well—those who lived righteous lives under the leading of the Holy Spirit will be proven right and acceptable to God. At the same time, those who refused the Good News of the gospel will be judged accordingly (1:8).

In expressing this positive picture of the reward for being faithful, Paul now draws on one of the most forceful images associated with Jesus in the Gospels—the kingdom of God. While Paul had referred in passing to the kingdom of God in his first letter to them (1 Thess. 2:12), here he uses the term the way Jesus used it—to demarcate clearly the two opposing realms of good and evil. And by their faithfulness and endurance he assures them they are "counted worthy of the kingdom of God" (1:5).

Before going on, we will understand the significance of Paul's reference to the kingdom of God at this point as we consider a most important fact, and one that is often forgotten by Christians of today. The Gospels—Matthew, Mark, Luke, and John—had not been written at the time Paul wrote his letters and when he mentioned the kingdom of God (see Rom. 14:17; 1 Cor. 4:20, 6:9, 15:24 and 50; Gal. 5:21). In spite of that, though, it seems that the traditions of Jesus' teaching about the kingdom of God were widely known.

A Parenthetical Note.

When we read and study the letters of Paul, we must try to visualize the time when there were no Gospels of Mark or John. There was nothing in writing about the traditions of Jesus—the first of the Gospels would come along a few years later. And so it was Paul, in these Thessalonian letters, who began the incredible task of putting down in writing some of the early church's testimony about the significance of the salvation Jesus brought to the world.

It is difficult for those of us who have grown up with our Bibles and New Testaments to think of Christians and a church that didn't have the Gospels. By the time we get to Paul's letters in our New Testament, we have been through the drama of the four Gospels and the book of Acts and are well prepared for Paul's teaching. But in the early church they depended on spoken stories of Jesus.

While the New Testament has a strong concern with the present experience of the Holy Spirit, Paul's teaching here refers to the future when those who have followed Christ will receive a reward of rest and glory (1:7). The idea of rest as Paul used it here is rooted in the Old Testament understanding of the Sabbath, especially as it is related to the seventh day of creation (Gen. 2:2–3). It is helpful in arriving at an understanding of this idea to know that rest in the

Rest and the Future.

Bible was not merely seen in terms of sleep. Rather, it was a time of refreshment and renewal.

This same thought is carried over into the New Testament. Here it is not to be interpreted in terms of death, cessation of life, or non-activity. Instead, the rest for Christians following the Second Coming of Christ and throughout all of what we call eternity will be a time of complete renewal and refreshment. The writer of the last book in our New Testament saw it this way, "And God shall wipe away all tears from their eyes; and there shall be no more death, neither sorrow, nor crying, neither shall there be any more pain" (Rev. 21:4).

On a recent talk show in Florida I was responding to telephone questions about the end of time. One gentleman with a horribly distorted view of the future said that he thought heaven would be a rather boring place, and he wouldn't enjoy going there.

While his attitude was a bit cynical, this idea is shared by a lot of people today. For many, heaven is a rich but dull, do-nothing place where partly disembodied people roam listlessly in a kind of "spaced-out" or trancelike state. I'll admit that such a view hardly sounds exciting or inviting. But it is not the Christian view.

The experience of God's "rest" is to be relieved from the weary struggles of life and to relax in the personal presence of a loving God—to enjoy the serenity of unselfish relationships and a frustration-free environment. Admittedly, symbols and picture language describing heaven are most inadequate. But when Jesus said, "And if I go and prepare a place for you, I will come again, and receive you unto myself; that where I am, there ye may be also" (John 14:3), I don't think He had in mind anything that would be boring. During Jesus' ministry, His enemies accused Him of many things, but no one ever said He was a bore.

The Revelation of Jesus.

Paul next moves on as he looks into the future and writes that "the Lord Jesus shall be *revealed* from heaven with his mighty angels" (1:7, italics mine). Now, as I have mentioned previously, Paul customarily used the Greek word *parousia* (presence) when referring to Jesus' Second Coming. Here, however, he uses another rather technical word translated "revelation"—the same Greek word from which we get the English term "apocalypse."

This change is quite purposeful. Paul wanted his read-

Excavations in Thessalonica showing a theater area and street. First-century sites are actually quite scarce in modern Thessaloniki, or Salonica, as it is generally known today. The original town on this site was known as Therme. But in 315 B.C., Cassander, the son of Alexander the Great, reestablished the city; he named it after Alexander's sister, Thessalonike.

ers to understand that at the great "revelation" of Jesus, He will be accompanied by "mighty angels"—by the "angels of his power." This expression is a familiar Hebraic way of emphasizing that the *power* of the angelic host was vested or located not in the angels but in God. And here now, such power is equally attributed to Jesus, God's Son!

By having introduced His appearance in this way, Paul is telling his readers of all time that Jesus is *the figure* of history to whom humankind is accountable. In other words, this Jesus was not only concerned with the future and the welfare of Christians who had suffered persecution, but He was also keenly aware of those who were responsible for the persecution. The Second Coming of Jesus is here pictured as a warning that judgment will be made on all of those who reject Christ and oppose His followers.

In Flaming Fire.

The awesomeness of this judgment scene is colorfully pictured by Paul's wording, "In flaming fire" (literally, "in a fire of flame") to describe the mysterious appearance of the Lord and His heavenly entourage. Readers of the different translations will find some variation here in terms of the placement of the wording and punctuation. We need not be confused by this when we remember that verse divisions and punctuation were added later. The earliest New Testament documents do not contain these features.

In general, the meaning of these words, though, is quite clear. The end-time appearance of Jesus will inspire either wonder or dread. It will be similar to the fear-inspiring appearances of God in the Old Testament. You will remember Moses with the burning bush (Ex. 3:2; see also Acts 7:30) and the fiery mountain (Deut. 5:4; see also Heb. 12:18–20), or Isaiah's statements about the fiery coal (Isa. 6:6–7), or Daniel's fiery judgment scene (Dan. 7:9–10). And while it is true that some of the fire references in our Bible emphasize cleansing (e.g., Isa. 6:6–7), many of them clearly portray the awe-inspiring God of righteous judgment. Indeed, the portraits of the Son of Man with fiery eyes, and the great angel with legs of fire as seen in Revelation 1:14, and the fire references of 3:18; 19:12; and 10:1, are all part of this same powerful literary motif that was used to depict the wonder of the Lord and His angels that will be seen at the time of final judgment.

A Sign to Non-Christians.

The image of fire not only reminds us of the awe-filled meetings with God as described in the Bible, it is also a powerful symbol in the New Testament of punishment for those who have lived wicked lives. We get a vivid sense of this symbolism in the image of the fire in hell (Matt. 5:22; 18:9; 25:41) and of the lake of fire (Rev. 19:20; 20:14–15; 21:8). And so we see that the fire image comes to us in a two-sided picture: The coming of Christ will not merely be a sign of Good News, but it will also be a sign of judgment and doom.

Paul now makes it clear in this part of our lesson (1:8) that God's condemnation will not be limited merely to those who are guilty of antagonistic and aggressive attacks on Christians. His point here is that those who refuse to accept and obey the gospel will be judged and condemned. Readers of Paul's letters down through the centuries have struggled with what he seems to be saying here—non-aggressive unbelievers will be judged in the same way as hostile persecutors of Christians.

The Question of Judgment.

To move the dilemma into the twentieth century, we might well ask, "Are those in Central and South America who have refused to accept Christ as their Savior as guilty as the men who have senselessly murdered missionaries? Are people who have rejected Christ in the Middle East as guilty as the terrorists who have killed hostages in cold blood?"

When we study carefully Paul's words in Romans 1:18–32, we see that all who reject God are guilty—even those who haven't heard directly as we have. Of these, Paul writes, "For the invisible things of him from the creation of the world are clearly seen, being understood by the things that are made, even his eternal power and Godhead; so that they are without excuse" (Rom. 1:20).

In other words, we understand from Paul's writings on this subject that he firmly believed that in God's eternal plans and purposes, everyone is made *aware* of God. But Paul here (1:8) focuses his discussion in terms of *action*. He is not speaking of intellectual ignorance when he writes, "Them that *know not* God" (italics mine). The Hebraic meaning of "knowing" or "to know" is not merely an intellectual phenomenon; it also involves a relational activity. This idea is well illustrated in Genesis 4:1, "And Adam *knew* Eve his wife; and she conceived..." (italics mine). Certainly, that kind of knowing is not an activity of the mind.

The Idea of Not Knowing.

From Paul's perspective of "knowing" as a relational activity, not "knowing" God meant not being properly related to Him—not obeying Him. Obedience was the relational activity Paul had in mind here—he links the knowledge of God with obeying the gospel of Jesus Christ.

*Eternal Judgment—
Separation from God.*

For Paul, a failure to know God relationally and a failure to follow and obey the Good News of the gospel were legitimate grounds for divine judgment (1:9). In explaining these severe words to his readers, Paul was echoing Jesus' own teaching—in referring to those who refused to *act out* the gospel He said, "And these shall go away into everlasting punishment" (Matt. 25:46).

Judgment isn't a message we particularly like to hear. But God would not be just and righteous if there were no consequences to wrong actions and behavior. He has provided through Christ's death and resurrection the means for our salvation, but if we reject them, we must then endure the consequences—eternal separation from God. It is disobedience that produces the eternal gulf that separates the unbeliever from God.

*Not a Time for Playing
Games with God.*

The tragic idea of people being separated from the presence and glory of God forever underlines the importance of living *now* for Him. Life here is not a time for playing games with God. To reject Christ and to mistreat our fellow human beings is to invite eternal disaster. To use another of Paul's metaphors, "Whatsoever a man soweth, that shall he also reap" (Gal. 6:7). We cannot avoid the consequences of our actions.

From these words of Paul, his Thessalonian readers were being reminded that God is just. God's love is not spineless. It is real and "earthy"; to ignore it invites serious consequences.

The Amazing Good News.

But then there is another side, for Paul now goes on to assure his readers that faithful believers will be rewarded (1:10). There is a glad day coming—the Second Coming of Christ. And at that time, everyone who has faithfully lived and acted out the Good News of Jesus Christ will share in and reflect the brightness and glory of the Lord. In a sense, we are in this life to be reflectors of Jesus, but in a far greater way that will be our role in that future of the new heaven and new earth.

This was amazing good news for Paul's first-century readers who were enduring extremely difficult times because of their faith in Christ. And in response to their central question, *all* believers, living or dead at the time of the

Lord's coming, will share in the wonder of that future life. Because of this reassuring good news their confidence in God and all He had for them could be enlarged.

At the same time, Paul's words are good news for us in our sophisticated technological twentieth century. To believe in God is to know that He is with us in the hard times as well as in the easy times. We can count on Him under every circumstance. To live for Him is an exciting adventure both now and in the future.

Paul's words here are clear. As Christians who love and serve the Lord as best we know how, we need have no fear of God's condemnation and judgment.

Paul now brings this section to a close by assuring the Thessalonian Christians that he and his missionary companions are praying for them (1:11–12), "We pray always for you." There is a captivating warmth and a caring concern expressed here that goes way beyond the use of words. He cared deeply for them and was proud of their faithfulness to their Christian commitment. Much feeling was expressed in his words here, and I'm sure his first-century readers could sense it even as we can.

Once again Paul models for us a passionate caring for his friends in Christ that we so desperately need today. Our fast-paced urban existence tends somehow to isolate us instead of drawing us together. We feel insecure and alone even in the middle of a crowd because we're not sure that anybody really cares for us. Loneliness drives people to the fringes of desperation and even suicide. But it is to this kind of world that Christ calls each of us to love and care for and pray for our struggling brothers and sisters in Him. It is true that as believers in Christ we are to be God-centered, but at the same time we are to be person-centered. For it is as we "reach out and touch someone" that we best serve the Lord.

It is in being faithful to our commitment, in loving God and our neighbors and through prayer and affirmation—building them up in the faith—that we come together as the family of God and offer glory and praise to Him (1:12). I have come to see that so many of the people we meet in shopping malls, in stores and offices, in our neighborhoods, and even in church have a great need to know that we are interested in them and care about them. But it isn't merely words they want to hear. Rather, they want to feel

Prayer Support (1:11–12)
An Assuring Word.

our presence and to know as Paul's readers did, that we care for them.

Finally, buried in the middle of verse 12 are the words, "In him." These words, "In Christ" and "In him" are a hallmark of Paul's letters. But Paul does not suggest that being "in Christ" involves a cloistered experience. Rather, we seem to sense in both his words and actions that we are to be "in Christ" at the crossroads of life—in church, in the store, in the home, in the office.

For the Christians at Thessalonica to know firsthand the power of being united with Christ even in the midst of their hard times was Paul's primary prayer concern. And this applies equally to us in our world. Our pressing need is to experience the wonderful sense of unitedness with our Lord and with our fellow Christians, and this unity of Spirit becomes possible through "the grace of our God and the Lord Jesus Christ" (1:12).

Lord, It is a privilege to abide in You. Help me to walk with You throughout the day to "practice Your presence." AMEN.

WHAT THIS SCRIPTURE MEANS TO ME
—2 Thessalonians 1:1–12

Thursday mornings are special times for me. My relational Bible study and prayer group meets then. I always need to be a part of a small group of struggling, growing Christians who are studying the Bible together and are holding each other accountable to God and His Story. I find that I constantly need to be reminded that God's Story takes priority over my story.

One morning last year nine of us gathered at the church for our weekly study time. Like field mice scurrying into a safe niche, we all raced in from frantic, busy lives to try to carve out some quality time with God.

When I looked at young Karen, I could see that she was about to explode with enthusiasm. I smiled because I recognized the signs. Karen always looked that way just before sharing her newest tale of doing business with God.

Last week Karen had told us about her latest rescue story. It was the Christmas season and Karen told how she had just pulled into the busy post office parking lot when she noticed a very old man unsuccessfully trying to cross the street to the Mall.

The street was jammed with cars and the impatient drivers ignored the old gentleman's attempts to cross. Without a moment's hesitation Karen walked over to the old man, slipped her arm through his and said, "We're gonna do this together." And gently she escorted him across the street without paying any attention to the blaring horns of the angry and impatient motorists.

When they reached the other side, she gave the relieved old man a hug and a kiss on the cheek and wished him a Merry Christmas. She then hurried back across the street, dodging the noisy cars, and finished her errands.

Later, when Karen arrived home that afternoon, she received a long-distance phone call with the news that her aged grandfather was dying. She was heartsick because there was no way she could see him before he died. But then, through her spiritual eyes, she saw that she really had said goodbye—when she walked the old gentleman across the street, had given him a hug and a kiss, and said, "Merry Christmas."

Now, in remembering that as I looked at Karen's expectant face, I wondered what God-story she would share with us today. Her "Let me tell you what happened!" quieted our buzzing voices, for we knew we were in for a treat. This is what she told us.

The day before, Karen and her small son, Christopher, had gone into McDonald's for a hamburger. While they were eating, she noticed a waitress who was somewhat retarded cleaning off a table. She was muttering to herself and tears were streaming down her face.

Karen walked over to her and said, "You're upset. May I help you?" The girl blurted out an answer, "I can't do all this work—empty the trash bins and clean off the tables. I need some help." And with that she broke out into shoulder-shaking sobs.

Tenderly, Karen said, "I used to work at McDonald's, and I know exactly what to do. Go bring me some large trash bags, then sit down and rest awhile."

For the next few minutes Karen emptied all the bins and cleaned off the tables. Then she walked over and gave the girl a hug. And with a big grin on her face, the girl said, "You've just given me my smile back."

After walking back to her table to rejoin Christopher, Karen felt a tap on her shoulder. Turning, she looked into the face of a bewildered man who asked, "Lady, do you know that girl? Is she a friend of yours?" Karen flashed a quick smile and replied, "Yes, and she's a friend of yours too. Don't you recognize her? She's a child of God."

When Karen had finished her story, there was not a dry eye in our group. Her obedience to God's command to "Love one another" had brought great joy to so many. To look at Karen now no one would believe that a mere two years ago she had been a hopeless and depressed alcoholic.

As I thought about Karen, I recalled vividly the words of Paul in the third verse of our lesson, "We are bound to thank God always for you, brethren, as it is meet, because that your faith groweth exceedingly, and the charity [love] of every one of you all toward each other aboundeth."

LESSON 7
2 THESSALONIANS 2:1—12

The End of Time

Dear God, In that day let me be found in You, awake and with my lamps trimmed. AMEN.

We come now in our studies to the key section of this second letter to the Thessalonian Christians. Also it is one of the most difficult to understand. Paul's picture language was undoubtedly clear to his first-century readers, but to those of us whose eyes and ears are attuned to twentieth-century images, the meaning is considerably more obscure.

It seems clear, though, that in these verses Paul's purpose is to once and for all correct their false ideas about the Second Coming of Christ and the end of time as we know it. There is every reason to believe from Paul's wording that he is building arguments here to support earlier teaching. Undoubtedly, Paul and his fellow missionaries were keenly disappointed that their earlier teaching and communications had not cleared up the distorted ideas the Thessalonian Christians had gotten about the events surrounding the end times.

Paul's Purpose.

The intensity of Paul's concern can be clearly seen in the opening words of our Scripture lesson when he writes, "Now we beseech you [beg you], brethren..." There is high drama in the intensity of feeling expressed here. And

The Thessalonian Misunderstanding (2:1–3a)
A Troubled Concern.

111

the reason for this intense concern comes through in verse 2, where we realize that Paul believes their understanding of the faith is not firm, that it is easily disturbed.

In his first letter Paul had tried to calm the Thessalonian Christians' feelings of insecurity over the future. We looked closely at this problem in Lesson 4. But because it is obvious that his first efforts had not been successful, Paul changes his approach. Now he "calls it like he sees it," and speaks more directly to their need.

A False Spiritual Word.

It would appear from the rest of Paul's wording in verse 2 that their "shaken and troubled minds" about the future came from three sources. The first of these was "by spirit." The word "spirit" here is not to be confused with the Holy Spirit. Rather this was Paul's way of identifying false information being communicated through some sort of "spiritual" knowledge or ecstasy. That idea may have come in worship as a prophetic word or as an interpretation of a tongues-speaking experience.

Now, Paul had made it clear earlier that the Thessalonian Christians should be attentive to prophetic teaching and to not inhibit the Holy Spirit in any way. But he had also given his readers instructions in the first letter to test or "Prove all things; hold fast that which is good" (1 Thess. 5:21). And certainly anything that "is good" would not be troubling or devisive.

And so the Apostle makes it clear here that even though what they had heard had seemed to be "by spirit," it was a "bad word"—it was in error. And error was to be avoided at all cost. Paul was ever gentle with new Christians, but he was decisive when it came to exposing error and fraud.

A False Spoken Word.

The second source of the troubling of their minds was "by word." This phrase, set in contrast to the "spirit," probably referred to some form of oral argument. The Greek word Paul used here is the familiar *logos*, from which our English world "logic" comes.

As you will recall from earlier discussions, the Greeks of the first century took great pride in their use of logic in oral persuasion and debate. They thoroughly enjoyed playing word games in their display of wisdom.

Apparently the insecure Thessalonian Christians had been susceptible to some false arguments and deviant ideas. It is possible they had fallen for these errant concepts simply because they were presented glibly and smoothly and had a "ring of truth." And so Paul denounced this false "word," even though it was couched in seeming logic.

Paul's warning here is as appropriate today as it was in the first century. Simply because a speaker is captivating and glib and uses the right buzz words doesn't mean that truth is being spoken. This is precisely why it is important that we study to be informed Christians. And that is why studies like the one we're doing together now are essential to our spiritual growth and maturity. How else can we know whether the words we hear are true or false?

Apparently, the third source of their troubled situation involved some form of written word that had come to them. This may have been a letter that claimed to have been from Paul himself—"Nor by letter as from us"—but he makes it clear that he was in no way responsible for it.

A False Written Word.

Most certainly, Paul wouldn't accept a falsehood or false teaching simply because it appeared in written form. After all, some things that are written simply aren't true. Believe me, anyone who has graded the term papers of students or has served as a newspaper editor—both of which I have done—quickly learns the meaning of the word "bilge" as it applies to some things that appear in written form. And even though some ideas may be "padded" or credited to someone who is a supposed authority, this in no way makes them acceptable and true.

But irrespective of the source or form of this "letter," even if it was credited to Paul, he wants them to understand that error or false teaching is not made acceptable or right simply because it is signed by someone in authority. And in this case, any value in connecting Paul's name to the false word fell flat because he would have nothing to do with supporting error. To put this idea into a framework that any high school student would understand: It doesn't make a wrong idea right to footnote it with a reference to some authority. Error is still error even if it is clothed in respectability.

We need now to take a closer look at the error that was polluting the thinking of the Thessalonian Christians. It was the persistent error that had plagued them before: a wrong understanding of the *parousia*—the Second Com-

The Error.

ing of Jesus—and of the great "gathering together unto him" that would occur at that time (2:1). But there was a slightly different twist to their problem now because some of them believed that the Lord was in the process of coming already, or that He in fact had come, "As that the day of Christ is at hand" (2:2). The Greek text of this section reads, "the day of the Lord is present [has come]."

The mid-first-century error about the Second Coming of Jesus that so disturbed some of the Christians in Thessalonica was just the beginning of a long history of speculations and miscalculations that have troubled the church for over 1,900 years. At various times, dates have been set and people have disposed of all their material goods in anticipation of Jesus' coming.

Other Christians have defuturized the Second Coming and have identified it with a personal spiritual experience. In fact, the time element in the Second Coming of Jesus has always been a difficult problem for Christians. To merge the "not yet" of Christ's coming into the "already" of Jesus' life on earth and our personal experiences has become a comfortable solution for some. Of course, in doing so the elements of final judgment and blessing fade into the background of the present. It is true that some balancing of good and evil may occur in our world in the course of time as we know it. But neither our clever logic nor the world order can solve the eternal problems of pain and injustice.

There are those, too, who have popularized an interpretation of the precise order and timing of each event that was thought to occur beginning with the Second Coming of Jesus. These views have been charted and linked with certain texts. And it is quite understandable from a human point of view that we want to know how and when future events will occur. And we may be particularly vulnerable during periods of physical or emotional pain because of our faith in our general tendency to tie all of our stresses to end time pain, persecution, and deliverance.

But the fact remains that in spite of certain signs and events, we do not know the hour or the day of Christ's coming. This will happen in God's time, not ours. In His time sin and evil will be judged and dealt with even as those who have been faithful to the Lord move into a New Day with Him. These are matters of God's concern and timing, not ours.

The important thing for us as Christians is to live for God in the present and not be deceived at any point by an easy or glamorous word about the end of time (2:3a). God will bring events to pass in line with His eternal purpose, and in justice He will deal appropriately with the evil in the world.

While the coming of Christ is in the hands of God, Paul definitely wanted his readers to understand that the end of time had not yet arrived. Indeed, it was almost as though Paul was providing in these verses a sign so that expectant Christians could mark that event.

The End of Lawlessness (2:3b–4)
A Quoted Sign.

The text of these verses, however, raises an interesting question because something seems to be missing. Apparently, though, these words (3b–4) are a quotation from some statement that was probably well known to Paul, and perhaps to his readers as well. But the quotation actually seems to begin in the middle of verse 3b. So, in order to make sense out of the context most translators have added an introductory statement, *"that day shall not come."* These words are not in the Greek text so they have been placed in italics. The original wording is simply, "because...unless the rebellion [apostasy] comes first," or as our King James text reads, "Except there come a falling away first."

Apostasy.

What are we to make of this intriguing text? Paul seems to be saying that before the Second Coming there will be a period or condition that is referred to in Greek as *apostasia*—a "falling away," a rebellion, which we take to be against Christ and His Church.

The Lawless One.

But now Paul goes on to compound our puzzle by writing that this rebellion would be epitomized in a person called "that man of sin." Other translations have referred to this person as the evil one or "the man of lawlessness" (2:3b). In introducing this Lawless One Paul once again used the technical term "revealed," from which we get the English word "apocalypse," to indicate his coming.

There seems little doubt from the way this reads that Paul intended his readers to contrast the revelation of this "Lawless One" with the revelation of the Lord Jesus (see also 2 Thess 1:7). In fact, later (2:9), Paul even mentioned the *parousia* (coming) of this Lawless One.

The comparison of this evil figure to Christ is obvious.

Jesus was the Obedient One (see for example Phil. 2:8), but this evil figure represents disobedience and disorder. Jesus was the fulfillment of the Law—the One who led obedient humanity beyond Law to a righteousness of faith (see Gal. 4:4–5; 5:14–18; Rom. 8:2–4; 10:4–5). But the concern of this evil figure was anarchy.

Then the role of this anarchist is further identified when immediately after introducing him as the Lawless One, Paul added that he is also "the son of perdition"—literally, "the son of destruction." This linkage of the man of lawlessness with destruction is a direct contrast with the saving role of Jesus in redemption. Christ's mission has always been to bring stability, wholeness, and integration into the world. But the mission of this Lawless One is the bringing of destruction, loss, confusion, and disintegration to the world.

The Forces in Our World.

At this point it may be helpful to remind ourselves of the various forces that are at work in our world. Some of these breed confusion, lawlessness, and hate. Others bring peace, integration, caring, and wholeness to life. As Christians, we need to pray for the mind of Christ in determining on the one hand what contributes to harmony and stability and on the other hand what is self-centered and actually promotes confusion and disintegration. But there are those counterfeits that can fool us. For example, the Marxist philosophy promises integration, but it actually promotes and feeds on confusion. Some Christians even do the same thing in the name of Jesus—they destroy peace and wholeness by insisting that everyone conform to their brand of "rightness." It is up to us "in Christ" to perceive the difference between what is genuinely Christian in the midst of the many counterfeits.

The Antichrist Figure.

With respect to counterfeit issues, writers and preachers have frequently identified this lawless figure as the Antichrist—the earthly opponent of Jesus Christ. Actually, the term "Antichrist" (singular) appears only in 1 John 2:18. Elsewhere (1 John 4:3 and 2 John 7) a number of antichrists seem to be in mind, suggesting that the opponents (plural) of Christ are considered to be antichrists. This same idea seems to be present in the Gospels where the term "false christs" or pseudo-christs is used (see Matt. 24:24 and Mark 13:22).

The Church of St. Sophia in present-day Thessalonica.

But all of this takes a somewhat different turn in the book of Revelation. Here the second beast that arose from the earth (Rev. 13:11–18) has been coupled by some teachers with a specific figure of the Antichrist from 1 John 2, although this term is not used in Revelation. But the fact that this beast seems to be a counterfeit lamb that performs powerful signs and bears the strange evil number 666, which was linked to Nero, the Roman emperor, lends support to the idea that Christians were anticipating the coming of one to the earth who would epitomize all opposition to Christ. It seems likely to me that Paul's identification of the "man of lawlessness" must have contributed significantly to the development of this idea of an opponent to Christ in the first-century church.

The Proud One.

Paul next gives us a rather colorful word picture that adds to our understanding of this "son of perdition," "Who opposeth and exalteth himself above all that is called God, or that is worshipped; so that he as God sitteth in the temple of God, shewing himself that he is God" (2:4).

Now, since we don't know for sure just all that Paul had taught the Thessalonian Christians previously, there may be some missing links in our chain of understanding. But it seems apparent that this son of destruction—this evil Man of Sin—not only sees himself as a super deity, but he also sees himself enthroned in the most holy place of the temple. This was a horribly distasteful idea for Paul, for he was well schooled in Jewish history and was intensely aware of those tyrants who weren't satisfied with being human rulers, but who insisted in taking on divine authority as well.

Historical Forerunners.

An early example of this kind of arrogance occurred during the Maccabean period when Antiochus IV, the ruler of Syria and conqueror of Israel, proclaimed himself to be god and was called "Epiphanes," which means "appearance of god." In one of his despicable fits he plundered Jerusalem around 168 B.C., slaughtered a pig on the sacred altar of sacrifice, and set up a statue of Zeus in the most holy place. The Jews never forgot that sacrilege, and when Judas Maccabeus reconquered Jerusalem in 165 B.C., they "cleansed" the temple of that terrible desecration. In celebration of that event they established the feast of Hannukah to mark the end of that horrible experience. Antiochus Epiphanes became to Jews and Christians alike a symbol of everything that was despicable and unholy.

But Paul and the first-century Christians had a much more up-to-date reminder of that same kind of evil and unholiness. The Roman Emperor Caligula had insane aspirations of deity, and in A.D. 39–40 he made plans to have his image enshrined in the temple of Jerusalem. While that never occurred, because of his death in A.D. 41, the very idea that it could happen gave Jews and Christians alike another illustration of the diabolical side of Rome. It was the negative view of Rome that prevailed at the time the book of Revelation was written, and Babylon—the bloodthirsty harlot—was symbolically portrayed as Rome (Rev. 17:5).

But even at this time of writing Paul seemed to sense that more trouble was coming. And he pictured that trouble in the form of a superpowerful, wicked person who was probably more evil than Antiochus and Caligula combined—the embodiment of doom!

A Relevant Insert (2:5–7)

While this Lawless One, this Man of Sin, had not yet appeared on the scene from Paul's point of view, he makes it clear (2:7) that there is no doubt about the presence of evil and lawlessness in the world and in Thessalonica. And so Paul now in these verses gives his readers of all time an insert in which he moves from a discussion of the future coming of the Man of Sin to how the present affects the future. In this insert Paul set out to make it clear to his readers the order of events in relation to the future. At the same time, Paul wanted them to understand that while it was true that no one knows when the Second Coming will occur, there are certain things that will happen before that climactic moment.

The Restrainer.

In verse 5 Paul reminds his readers that he had talked about these things when he was with them. We don't know exactly how he worded his original discussion, so we are dependent in our understanding on what he is writing here.

His point is clear: Future events are being forestalled because of the presence of he that "withholdeth" (2:6). Other translations refer to this one as "the restrainer," the one who is holding evil back, or the one who is now restraining evil. A free translation of the original Greek might well be, "The one or the thing who (which) restrains or checks." And so, the next logical question is: Who is this restrainer, or what is this restraining force that keeps certain events still in the future?

Some Possibilities.   Of immediate significance is that the Thessalonian Christians themselves apparently knew what Paul was saying. And so he simply says in verse 6 that there was no need for him to elaborate further. Unfortunately for us in the twentieth century, the meaning is not clear.

Some have suggested that the restrainer of evil is God or Christ, but that doesn't seem to fit with Paul's wording here. Others have argued strongly that the restrainer is the Church and that the Lawless One would be unleashed when the Church is taken out of the world. But I don't believe that idea fits into Paul's thinking about the events of the End Time either.

The most natural meaning would be to interpret the "withholder" or "restrainer" as an oblique reference to the power of Rome. Because of the form of the original wording Paul could have had in mind either the empire or the emperor as being the restraining force because it would appear he still had a positive feeling about the power of the state to preserve order (see also the implication of his comments in Rom. 13:3–4).

But this idea certainly presents a problem from our point of view because the Roman Empire ended long ago and the Lawless One has seemingly not put in his appearance. Such being the case, this opens up the possibility that Paul might have implied a generalized view of "government" as the restrainer of evil and anarchy. But that doesn't seem to fit the context of Paul's thinking either. So the specifics continue to be obscure.

That may cause problems for some Christians. But there's much about God's eternal purposes that in our humanness we need to leave up to Him. Throughout history, since the first century, there have been evil persons and powers that have threatened the world scene for a time, but in every case there has been a restraining force that has prevented disaster.

Out of all of the examples I might cite I'll mention just two or three to make the point. As the armies of the Union and the Confederacy moved toward the close of what we know as the Civil War or the War Between the States, there were those vindictive persons in the north who wanted to "punish" the south—to take advantage of and plunder the "enemy." But General Grant and President Lincoln were the "restrainers." Among other gestures of amnesty, General Grant permitted the defeated southern soldiers to take their horses home to pull the plows on their farms and plantations.

In the 1930s and early 1940s Hitler threatened the sanity of the world, and his armies swept across Europe as if nothing could stop them. But the United States and the Allied Armies became the "restrainers" that in time turned the tide and defeated the intentions of evil.

Every century has had its forces and people of evil, but every century has also had its restrainers that prevented evil from prevailing. Future events will fall into place according to God's timing in spite of speculations.

Paul looks ahead now to that time when the restraining power or person is removed from the world—a time when literally all hell breaks loose. Then the coming and actions of the Lawless One will be directed by none other than Satan himself (2:9). The functions of this Lawless One remind us of the two terrible beasts of Revelation 13, which are to arise and serve the great dragon, a symbol of Satan, the opponent of God. The Lawless One, according to Paul, will exert false or counterfeit power, signs, and wonders (2 Thess. 2:9; see also Mark 13:22) in much the same way that the false lamb will operate in the symbolic vision of Revelation 13:13. And the Lawless One's distinct purpose under the direction of Satan will be to deceive those who will be destroyed (2 Thess. 2:10; see also Rev. 13:14–15).

The End of the Lawless One and His Followers (2:8–12)
A Link with Revelation.

Deception is a classic function of evil, and the basic style of evil is selfishly self-assertive. The powers of evil are fully capable of copying certain aspects of the good in order to confuse the unenlightened and to persuade them to move forward on a destructive path.

Paul understood this phenomenon of deception very clearly, and he likened the Lawless One to a deceptive imitator or copycat of the Lord Jesus. Not only does he have a *parousia* (coming) like Christ, but he performs pseudo-miracles that will deceive all except those who have committed themselves to the Lord (2:9–12).

The classic purpose of evil is to divert worship from God to some pseudogod. Sometimes the differences, though

The Deception of Evil.

121

critical, are extremely subtle. To prevent being deceived, the Christian needs insight and wisdom and a spiritual maturity that is able to recognize the true faith.

Paul's message to his Thessalonian friends and us today is that the power to perform what appear to be miracles is not a sign that the performer is necessarily a God-sent person. Rather, we need the insight that can be provided only by the Holy Spirit to look behind the performance to the motive.

At the same time, we need the spiritual discernment to understand that evil may frequently present the inviting appearance of being a positive force in the economical or social structure of society or in the religious realm. But to the sensitive and Spirit-filled Christian, evil is evil even if it is spoken or acted out in the name of God.

Paul then goes on to assure his readers that evil and evil persons will be judged and rewarded according to their evil actions (2:11–12). This is the only possible response from a just God to those who have deliberately chosen to accept error and believe the lie—the denial of the truth of God—and reject the Savior. And verse 12 affirms that those who have turned their backs on the will and purposes of God will in turn be rejected by God.

A Final Word.

As was mentioned earlier, we have been working through some extremely difficult verses in this particular lesson. In a sense, we've been attempting to arrive at some answers while having access to only one side of a conversation. But in general, Paul's message is clear: We are not to be deceived by false teaching of any kind about the Second Coming of Christ and the end of time.

Paul assured his first-century readers that the end had not yet arrived. And for us in the twentieth century—the end has not yet arrived. But it is coming! In the meantime, of this we can be sure—even though conditions in our world may seem hopeless and even though evil may appear at times to have won the day, God will not let Satan and the forces of evil triumph. The final victory belongs to God and to all who love the truth and are saved (2:10).

The confidence that we can have as Christians who are committed to Jesus Christ is that He will walk through every hour of our day with us in the down-to-earth world in which we live now. And when that Day of the Lord

comes—whenever it is—we will begin a new life with the
Savior in a new world.

To God be the glory, for our ultimate victory is secure in
Him and in His Son, Jesus our Lord!

*Lord God, Thank You for walking through my day with me. I appre-
ciate Your presence—and I need it. AMEN.*

WHAT THIS SCRIPTURE MEANS TO ME
—2 Thessalonians 2:1—12

In this lesson Paul was trying to still the frantic cries and questions of the Thessalonian Christians. They were spending much of their valuable "now" moments in great
apprehension, confusion, and concern over the End Times and the Second Coming of Jesus. These verses remind me of an incident that happened to my husband, Chuck.

It was a blustery, bleak day. Chuck was hurrying to avoid being late on his first
visit to a men's noontime Bible study group. Upon arriving at the meeting place,
he walked into a room filled with chatter and a clutter of brown bags and ther-
mos bottles.

Chuck knew that these men had been involved in a study of the book of Revelation for five years. And it soon became obvious from the lively discussion that they
were really caught up in the mystery and puzzling symbols of the book.

With passion they attempted to unravel the secrets of John's apocalyptic writing. One man shared a new insight about the identity of the woman with the moon
at her feet and another read a scholarly paper about the beast from the sea. They
all seemed mesmerized by their speculations on the meaning of the colorful
language.

Since all of the men were on their lunch hours, it was important that the meeting end promptly. It was almost time to go when one of the men who had been
exceptionally quiet bolted to his feet and blurted out, "Would you please pray for
me? You see, I got fired today." And overcome with emotion he rushed out of
the door.

Chuck told me the silence in that room was deadening. There were embarrassed glances passing among the men as first one and then another said, "If we had only known!" "Why didn't he speak up sooner?" "Who would have ever suspected that Barry's job was in jeopardy?" "What can we do now?" But the time was gone and each man drifted back to his own work day agenda. With a troubled heart, Chuck, too, returned to work with the realization that a wonderful opportunity to minister to a brother had been lost—had slipped through the cracks.

I'll admit I usually find it much more comfortable to study and analyze Scripture on forgiveness than I do to move into the real world of forgiving a friend. It is easier to get caught up in speculation about John's mysterious words in Revelation than to hear Jesus' confronting words, "Love one another." Now, don't misunderstand, studying God's Word is important, but it is also important that we live out the Word in a practical and loving way that speaks to the needs and hurts of our family and friends.

Lord, through Your grace, and Your Holy Spirit, help me give my 'now' moments to you. Give me a passion to learn of You, and then to sense a great restlessness until I put Your words into action—for both of our sakes! Amen.

LESSON 8
2 THESSALONIANS 2:13–3:18

A Concluding Charge

Heavenly Father, Help me to be "stedfast, unmoveable, always abounding in the work of the Lord." AMEN.

While the concluding remarks in both of the Thessalonian letters focus on some very practical matters of living, there is a marked difference in emphasis. In the first letter (Lesson 5) Paul mentioned briefly a number of rather general exhortations that covered a fairly wide range of issues related to Christian living.

Now, however, as Paul moves toward the close of this letter, he is much more specific as he focuses on his concern for steadfastness from several perspectives.

The Foundation for Endurance (2:13–17)

Up to now in this follow-up letter Paul has reminded his readers that even though they were having to endure some very hard times of persecution because of their faith in Christ, their confidence must remain securely fixed in God. He next attempted to correct their wrong understanding of the Second Coming of Christ and the end of time as we know it. And now he moves on to focus their attention on the need for them to experience a renewal of confidence and faithfulness to their Christian commitments.

The Thanksgiving Theme.   Paul returns now to the thanksgiving theme which he introduced at the beginning of the letter (1:3), "We are bound to give thanks alway to God for you" (2:13). But the emphasis is somewhat different here as compared to the first prayer of thanksgiving. In the first instance he was thanking God for the development of their faith. Here, however, in addition to being thankful for *their* faith, Paul and his missionary friends are expressing thanksgiving for the fact that the Thessalonian Christians are *loved by God*.

Loved by God.   What a marvelous word of affirmation for the Thessalonian Christians—*they are loved by God*. This is the first part of the wonderful summation of the gospel of Jesus Christ that Paul gives his readers here (2:13–17). And the core of that Good News is that God loves us.

Those beleaguered Christians in Thessalonica were being abused and persecuted because of their faith in God. Paul doesn't mean to say that their neighbors were irreligious. Not at all. But their faith was in many gods, including the emperor in Rome. And they had no time or patience for those Christian disturbers who worshiped God only through Christ. And because the Thessalonian Christians were feeling isolated and alone they needed to be reminded—as Paul does here—of the Good News that God loves them.

And this reminder was especially important here following immediately on Paul's discussion of judgment for sin.

Most certainly, the heart of the gospel is that God loves people. He loves the helpless, the poor, the hungry, the affluent, the brilliant, the retarded. God's love is color-blind and knows no geographical or national boundaries. It takes in everybody, including you and me and those people around us we have a hard time getting along with.

Yes, as Paul has been writing, God opposes and judges sin and the evil one. But more importantly, He so loved the world that He opened the way for us to find forgiveness, hope, and acceptance through Jesus Christ. The love of God is the very foundation of our salvation through Christ.

Chosen by God.   Paul now speaks of the next feature of the gospel in his summary, "God hath from the beginning chosen you to salvation" (2:13). This has the same ring as Paul's words to the Ephesian Christians, "He hath chosen us in him before the foundation of the world" (Eph. 1:4). The apostle is stressing the truth that our faith in God and His love for us doesn't rest on any kind of flimsy foundation of frail human choices. God has chosen us to be His sons and daughters.

This idea, though, of God's choosing, has raised a question in the minds of people for years: If God chooses some for salvation, does that mean that He chooses others for destruction? Of course not! The choosing of God is not for the selfish purpose of benefitting only a few. Rather, it is God's way of delivering the message of salvation to the whole world. To be chosen is not an end in itself, but it is a part of God's great plan of providing hope for the entire world. God has chosen some so that all will have the opportunity to know and experience His love.

First Fruits.

We need to take a further look at what Paul seems to be saying in verse 13. Instead of reading "from the beginning God chose you" some manuscripts read, "God chose you as his first fruits." The difference in Greek is merely the way the letters of the words are divided. I happen to feel there is much in favor of this latter idea.

It seems likely to me that Paul is telling his readers that they—the Thessalonian Christians—have been chosen as the first fruits of God in their area of Macedonia. It is true that the first Christians in Macedonia were in Philippi. But in terms of first-century travel, Philippi was a long way from Thessalonica. And as the capital city of Macedonia, Thessalonica had tremendous influence in that area.

The concept of the "first fruits" is very much an Old Testament idea in which the first fruits of a harvest were dedicated to God in behalf of the whole harvest. Paul may well be suggesting to his readers that they are indeed the first fruits of God's work in their region. And as such, they carry a heavy responsibility in their witness for the Lord.

The Process of Salvation.

Paul now goes on in verse 13 to write that they have been "chosen...*to salvation* through sanctification of the Spirit and belief of the truth" (italics mine). As I explained earlier, when Paul used the term salvation, he had much more in mind than that first step of faith in which the believer is made right in God's sight. Rather, he had the entire process of new *life* in mind. In addition to including belief in the truth, it also includes the process of being sanctified or made holy by the Holy Spirit (2:13).

And then Paul goes on to say that the process of salvation would not be completed until it included the final stage when they gained or laid hold of or became participants in the magnificent "glory of our Lord Jesus Christ" (2:14). The sanctification Paul is writing about here is part of the salvation process and is the work of the Holy Spirit here and now, but it will be completed at the Second Coming of Christ.

Called by the Gospel.

It was to this complete message of salvation that Paul felt called, and he reminds his readers in verse 14 that they, too, are called to witness to this same message. This call is equally strong for us in these closing years of the twentieth century. There is nothing casual about an authentic commitment to Jesus Christ.

First, we are to be open to receiving all that God has for us in the salvation process. And then we are to share this same message and experience with the people around us. As Paul saw it and as he lived it, our call is for an all-out, energized commitment to Christ.

Clinging to the Traditions.

Paul next makes a strong appeal to his readers, "Therefore, brethren, stand fast, and hold the traditions which ye have been taught, whether by word, or our epistle" (2:15). He seems to be saying here that traditions are the bedrock of the church. In fact, Paul emphasized his point by telling them to have an iron-fisted grasp on those traditions.

Paul's use of the word "traditions" here can create some questions with many Christians—especially those who think of the term in a negative sense. It is true Paul used the term in a negative sense when he told the Christians in Colossae to "Beware lest any man spoil you through philosophy and vain deceit, after the tradition of men, after the rudiments of the world, and not after Christ" (Col. 2:8). And the same idea is implied when both Jesus and Paul

A statue of Augustus Caesar in the museum at Thessalonica. Augustus was Emperor of the Roman Empire from 27 B.C. to A.D. 14.

contrasted the traditions of the Jewish elders or rabbis with the actions or the Word of God (Matt. 15:1–6 and Gal. 1:14).

On the other hand, though, tradition had a very positive side for Paul. After all, he had been trained in the schools of the rabbis, and he had learned well the thought patterns and language forms of those schools. They served him well, and it is obvious from his writings that this educational background had made an indelible impression on him.

The impact of Paul's rabbinical training can be seen in his understanding of how to pass along the traditions. His words in 1 Corinthians 15:1–3 are a superb illustration of correct traditional thinking. When he wrote here about the basic Christian affirmations related to the death and resurrection of Jesus, he used the terminology of the rabbis for the passing on of tradition: The Corinthian Christians had "received" and were "established" (stand) firmly (15:1) because Paul had "delivered" (handed over) what he himself had "received" (15:3).

In line with typical rabbinic training, students were to "deliver" *unchanged* to others what they had "received" or what had been passed on to them. The very term "deliver" in Greek is directly related to the Greek word for "tradition."

Now, when Paul became a Christian, the shift for him was not in the way he viewed the "passing along" of tradition, but the source of the tradition. As a former rabbi, Paul's sources had been the great teachers of the past. But now, Jesus Christ was the source of Paul's tradition. And he is telling his readers to stand firmly for the traditions about Jesus that he had given them before.

It is true, of course, that tradition has a negative and narrow form when it is used as an umbrella for the idea "that we do something because it has always been done that way before." It is that kind of excuse that is always "hanging onto the tail of progress and shouting 'whoa'." Clinging to negative tradition and forms can so easily be a cover-up for resistance to creative change.

On the other hand, we are blessed with almost 2,000 years of Christian tradition, beginning with our New Testament and continuing with the witness of outstanding and ordinary Christians and the church. The accumulated wisdom and experience that has been passed on to us through the centuries can and should be a great reservoir of spiritual truth that can enrich our lives as we in turn "pass along" the great traditions of what it means to live *for Christ*.

Having completed his "stand fast" admonition, Paul now expressed his loving concern for his readers in the form of a hopeful prayer of comfort. In this prayer we have an affirmation of God's love, of His continual encouragement, and of the hope we have in Him (2:16–17). And so Paul is praying that his first-century readers in the capital city of Thessalonica will experience personally these affirmations and be firmly established in their faith and not be continually troubled by a false understanding of the gospel.

A Hopeful Prayer.

It is in prayers like this that we catch the love and tenderness in the heart of Paul. He had hoped in his first letter to correct the error that had cast an ominous pall over the Thessalonian church. But the error persisted, and now he has written a second letter. Each letter has addressed their deviation from what he had taught them, and he has called them to a renewed commitment now to the correct traditions. But we find no ring of impatience here—no touch of anger. Rather, Paul remains tender and thoughtful as he prays for them and writes to them.

Paul's Tenderness.

What a marvelous transformation in the life of this flaming zealot of Judaism who had formerly condemned and imprisoned early Christians for their deviation from the Jewish faith. When Paul became a Christian, he continued to have little tolerance for error, but the love of God in Christ exposed a tender side that enabled him to be the mighty "convincer" for Christ that he had become.

Once again, Paul has modeled for us here Christ-like attitudes and actions that are so appropriate for us as we attempt to live out our faith in our complex world. Yes, it is always important that we "stand fast" for the truths of our faith. But it is equally important that we "stand fast" in a spirit of love and acceptance. So often Christians appear angry and manipulative in their "defense of the faith." This was not the model Christ gave us. And it certainly does not mirror the spirit of Paul. He obviously had never forgotten the harshness and vindictiveness of his pursuit of "error" before he met Christ on the Damascus road. His patience,

A Model for Us.

his tenderness, and his tact remain for us a model of gentleness.

A Two-Sided Prayer for Endurance (3:1–5)

Paul opens Chapter 3 of this letter by saying, "Finally." This was not to imply that he was now finished, but rather that he had covered his main points and was now ready to move toward the conclusion. He still, though, has some important and instructive words for them.

The Human Side of Paul and His Fellow Missionaries.

Paul first makes a very moving request for prayer for himself and his missionary associates. Along with Silvanus and Timothy, Paul was constantly giving of himself to encourage and support the new Christians. They had done this in person at Thessalonica and were now giving of themselves vigorously to the church at Corinth. We can almost at times feel their exhaustion creeping into their words. Admittedly, they weren't superhuman—the pressures were extremely great.

And so they ask, "Pray for us" (3:1). It is interesting, though, as we look at these verses, that they didn't ask for relief from the pressures and persecution merely for the sake of being delivered from them. After all, Paul had learned already that he could not escape from the attack of those who opposed him. Instead, Paul goes on to pray that "the word of the Lord may have free course." Once again Paul seems to be using the race metaphor, for the idea seems to be that the unhindered Word of God will run quickly and will spread rapidly.

There's a hint in these words of the athletic language that became so much a part of Paul's later descriptions of the missionary task and the struggle for salvation (see also for example, Rom. 9:16; 1 Cor. 9:24–27; Gal. 2:2 and 5:7; Phil. 2:16).

And then in verse 2 Paul requests prayer specifically that they "may be delivered from unreasonable and wicked men." We get a hint here of a similar thought in the Lord's Prayer, "Deliver us from evil" or from the "evil one." But it is also likely that Paul had in mind those persons who were hindering the gospel by their opposition—in Thessalonica, in Corinth, and even in Jerusalem.

The Importance of Prayer.

Throughout all of Paul's letters we catch his strong emphasis on the importance of prayer in the life of the Christian. Unfortunately, though, this is an exercise in our

Christian pilgrimage which is too often neglected. And then when we do pray, we have the tendency to treat God as some sort of cosmic bellboy. We pray for something we desperately want or to get out of some crisis situation.

But again and again Paul stresses the importance of praying *for each other*—praying that our fellow Christians will have the guidance they need, will be touched physically, will have the strength to make it through a time of testing. Then, too, we have a Christian responsibility to pray for those who carry the weight of governmental leadership—mayors, members of Congress, senators, ambassadors, the president, and all who are trying to negotiate peace across the world. And we are to pray that "the word of the Lord may have free course" and that it will reach all who "have not faith."

Martin Luther summed it all up when he wrote, "Prayer is a powerful thing, for God has bound and tied himself thereto. None can believe how powerful prayer is, and what it is able to effect, but those who have learned it by experience."

Evil and the Power of God.

Scarcely had Paul concluded his request for prayer than he turned again to remind his readers of the overwhelming faithfulness of the Lord in guarding and protecting them from the evil one (3:3). As in the Lord's Prayer (Matt. 6:13), the original language isn't clear as to whether "evil" is masculine or neuter. But given Paul's belief that Satan is behind all evil activity (see 2 Thess. 2:9), the translational variance makes little difference. Evil for Paul is not some impersonal force in the universe. Instead, evil is the result of a determined will set against God. But again and again we have the assurance that determined evil cannot overcome the Lord's firm and secure power.

A Prayer for Love and Stability.

Once again Paul affirms his Thessalonian friends, but he makes it clear that his confidence is based on the Lord's control of their lives (3:4), and their being in the center of His will. And he prays first that the love of God will be the motivating force in their lives and that they will discover true stability (3:5).

Paul's insightful prayer for his readers is a response to their troubled spirits as they face difficulties and persecution on one hand, and disturbing ideas on the other (see 2 Thess. 2:2). He wants them to see that the answer to their difficulties is not to be found in their own resources, but in the stabilizing presence of the living Christ in their lives.

Once again the application seems clear. Our world is caught in a horrible vise of turmoil, suspicion, misunderstanding, and the threat of violence and war. Children are dying of starvation while farmers are paid not to raise crops. People are denied their human rights because of color, and brothers are fighting brothers. The answer to these vicious dilemmas is not to be found in our human resources, but in the power of God through the love of Christ. Stability can come only as God changes the hearts of people—and He can.

Responsible Christian Living (3:6–15)

Paul's Drive.

We have no way of knowing for sure whether Paul was a "Type A" personality or not, but he certainly seems to have been a man driven by a powerful sense of purpose. Passionate people like Paul make a tremendous difference in our world. They are the doers and shakers. And when Paul met Jesus Christ, he found a channel for his zeal that regulated the rest of his life.

There is just no way I can picture Paul having much patience with anyone who was irresponsible or playing at being a Christian. When Paul had first met the Lord, the change in his life was drastic, and I'm sure he expected the same kind of change in the life of every new Christian. I can just imagine that one sure way to get Paul excited was to say, "Come on, Paul, don't get so worked up about Jesus." There was nothing halfway or lukewarm about Paul's commitment. He was an all-or-nothing kind of person.

Christian Sponges.

And certainly anyone with Paul's personality would have been outraged by the thought of any Christian refusing to work and sponging on others. It would have made little difference whether that person felt that work was below his dignity or that the Second Coming of Jesus was just around the corner. He reminds his readers here in verse 10 that he had urged them to keep working when he was with them. He repeated this admonition in his first letter to them, and now he comes on strong by saying, "If any would not work, neither should he eat" (3:10).

Some interpreters of these verses have twisted things to suit their own purposes by implying that Paul was laying down a philosophy of work here that applied under every

A collection of figurines and pottery of Macedonian origin on display at a museum in Thessalonica.

situation. I don't think so. But let's stop a moment and look into the setting again.

Remember, the Thessalonian Christians were members of a young church that was struggling toward maturity in a pagan and hostile society. Within their congregation Paul says there are those who are "disorderly" (KJV). Certain other translations refer to these as being "idle." Either way, the reference here is to undisciplined and disorderly conduct. It was Paul's concern here that the Thessalonian Christians be disciplined, exemplary citizens who would go about their work quietly and not disturb society (3:12). He knew that their witness would be more powerful if they would use their energy to do things that created positive results in society (3:13).

The Issue of Discipline.

Disorderly Types. Apparently the majority of the Thessalonian Christians understood Paul's instructions, but some didn't. They were the disorderly types who were deliberately busy doing the wrong things. Paul called them "busybodies." They were so busy trying to mind everybody else's business that they completely neglected their own. They were troublemakers who were using the church as a setting for their own selfish benefit—like pirates, they were feeding off the work of others and giving the Christian community a bad reputation.

Irresponsible and undisciplined behavior in the first century or the twentieth reflects on the Christian community. How often have we heard someone say, "If that is Christianity, I don't want any part of it."

Paul's Answer. This was the situation Paul was responding to here, and he met it head-on with all the authority he felt was his as an apostle, "Now we *command* you, brethren, in the name of our Lord Jesus Christ, that ye withdraw yourselves from every brother that walketh disorderly" (3:6, italics mine). That was strong and to the point, and there was no way his readers could misunderstand what he wanted them to do.

We know from our studies so far that Paul didn't make a habit of insisting on his authority as an apostle of the Lord unless he was pushed. It hardly meant that he was unaware of his rights (3:9), but he wouldn't take advantage of them. And as a case in point, he reminds the Thessalonian Christians that when he and his missionary associates were with them they didn't take support but worked "night and day" so as not to be a financial burden to the young church. He wanted them to see that in working as they had, he and his friends had provided a model of what it meant to be self-giving and orderly Christians. And he now makes it clear that he expected them to copy or imitate the life-style he and his associates had modeled (3:7, 9).

It is quite likely that while most of the Thessalonian Christians heeded Paul's message and modeled their lives after that of the missionaries, there were those who refused to follow instructions. For these, Paul recommended shock treatment, "And if any man obey not our word by this epistle, note that man, and have no company with him, that he may be ashamed. Yet count him not as an enemy, but admonish him as a brother" (3:14–15).

Once again, Paul seems to be exerting his authority as an apostle. He is instructing the church to isolate these busy-bodies and troublemakers from the intimacy of the community as a means of making them feel ashamed. In other words, by avoiding those who were creating dissension in the church by their actions, it was hoped that they would amend their disruptive ways.

At the same time, though, they were not to regard such offenders as hostile outsiders. They were still brothers who needed to recognize the error of their ways. The picture we get here is of an action being taken not to alienate, but to correct and discipline disruptive activities within the church—an action taken in genuine love.

The Need for Models of Love.

I think Paul's attitude here is extremely important for us as members of the community of faith. We know, of course, that there may be those isolated instances where extreme measures of discipline are called for when situations occur like those in Corinth (1 Cor. 5:1–13). But for the most part our differences within the church fellowship take on a less severe form. And at such times we would do well to take a page out of Paul's book and not treat those we differ with like enemies, but as brothers and sisters in Christ.

Paul's love-model in Christian attitudes and relationships is greatly needed today. There is such a need for our non-Christian neighbors to see and feel the love of Christ in the lives of those who profess Him. But all too often they see what I did recently when I was sick with the flu over a weekend—angry looking and sounding preachers on television and radio whose style and spirit didn't seem to square with their words. Then, too, there are those frequent news reports of infighting and name-calling within the church. These reports only serve to alienate unbelievers.

Beyond that, though, the buck ultimately passes right on down to Christians like those of us who are studying these lessons together. The Lord wants us to be models of love to our neighbors next door and across the street, to people in the office or in the bank or department store, to the checker at the grocery counter. Do they "know we are Christians by our love?"

The Conclusion (3:16–18)

Peace.

As Paul begins now to end this important letter, he gives his readers of all time this twofold prayer. The first movement of this short prayer speaks of peace, "Now the Lord of peace himself give you peace always by all means" (3:16a). This wording is a bit unusual because normally Paul referred to the "God of peace," as he did in the first letter (5:23). But the emphasis on the expected Second Coming of Jesus may have been in the forefront of his mind as he dictated these closing words.

To anyone of a Hebrew and Semitic background the word "peace"—*shalom*—had great meaning then and it does now. Whether at the beginning or end of a conversation, *shalom* is a pleasantry that is always expected.

Christian Peace.

But this part of Paul's prayerful greeting was much more than a polite pleasantry. It was his wish that Christians of all times and in all situations would experience the wonderful peace that is made available by God in Jesus Christ.

The word "peace" has become a byword in the give-and-take of our twentieth-century life—peace among individuals and among nations. But the peace you and I need to strive for and pray for is the one that comes through an encounter and intimate relationship with the Prince of Peace.

The Lord's Presence.

The second part of this short prayer reads simply, "The Lord be with you all" (3:16b). The fact of Christ's presence with the believer is a vital part of the magnificent message of the gospel. It brings to mind the reassuring words of Jesus to His disciples after the resurrection, "Lo, I am with you alway" (Matt. 28:20). And many years before Matthew wrote his Gospel we have Isaiah's reference to the coming of Jesus (Isa. 7:14), which Matthew quoted, "Behold, a virgin shall be with child, and shall bring forth a son, and they shall call his name Emmanuel, which being interpreted is, *God with us*" (Matt. 1:23, italics mine).

This was powerful news to the beleaguered Thessalonian Christians in the first century, even as it is to us now. The risen Lord is with us, and He wants to occupy every "room" in our lives—to be a part of all of our words and actions. It is this transforming Presence that Paul wants his readers to experience.

Paul's Certification.

Paul now senses the need to assure his readers that he is the author of this letter (3:17). Rather than merely signing a letter as we do today when a secretary has typed it for us, people in Paul's day often took the pen from the scribe and added a brief sentence or a mark that would be recognized by the reader. It was a symbol that the letter was genuine. As Paul writes in verse 17, this is a practice that he followed "in every epistle."

Paul may well have felt that this reassurance was essential because of the false teachers who tried to lead the church astray (2:3). He knew the importance of each letter in the life and development of the Christians to whom he was writing. He wanted his readers to know without question that the words they were reading were his.

A Final Word.

Paul closes this letter now almost identically to the way he closed the first one, "The grace of our Lord Jesus Christ be with you all. Amen" (3:18). From beginning to end Paul knew that life in Christ was a matter of grace.

Paul and Silvanus and Timothy opened this remarkable letter with an emphasis on grace, and now they close it the same way. It is the grace of God that brackets all that we are and have; it is the heart of the Good News.

The central thrust of this second letter to the Thessalonian Christians was to further correct their false ideas about the Second Coming of Jesus and how they should live before He returns. Having studied it a little over 1,900 years later, we have become keenly aware that certain mistaken attitudes and speculation that existed then are still with us.

But as Christians, we still live in anticipation of that wonderful time in the unknown future when Christ will come again and God's new world order will become a reality. Yet for now, our primary task is to live twenty-four hours of every day as members of God's great new society in this real world—in the cities, towns, and neighborhoods where God has put us to be His witnesses.

Father God, Your grace "taught my heart to fear, and Your grace my fears relieved." Thank You Father for Your beautiful, limitless grace. AMEN.

WHAT THIS SCRIPTURE MEANS TO ME
—2 Thessalonians 2:13–3:18

The words, "Brethren, do not be weary in well doing," leap out at me as I'm reminded of one particular morning a few years ago. Frazzled and exhausted from tyring to be a dutiful minister's wife, mother, daughter, speaker, friend, and child of God, I felt all used up. I remember thinking, "Lord, I'm so tired of the stretching, growing, and groaning that comes from trying to be Your person. Can't you just pass me by and give all my assignments to someone else?" And with that off my chest, I sat down to put my feelings at that moment on paper.

"Lord, when I'm weary from well doing and from the stress of life's pilgrimage, I discover a comfortable plateau, a resting place—a place where I've learned all the landmarks and shortcuts. I know where the chugholes are, the way the rivers flow, and I want so much to stay right there and relax. In the stress of the moment I cry, 'Lord, I have really done much more than my share. I've gone through uncharted lands with only You as guide. Being an adventurer and an explorer is just not my nature. And not knowing the end of the script confounds and confuses me.'

"Many times on my life-journey I've been bruised by rough places. The sky has been so black and foreboding. There were no moon or stars to light my way, and You seemed to have disappeared completely. Yes, it is true You always found me in the midst of those dark moments—but it was always Your time, not mine.

"And so, Lord, I'd like to stay right here on this pleasant and undemanding plateau. Please just give my game plan to someone else. I'm tired of growing, stretching, stumbling, and getting entangled in the many jungles along the way. I'm wearying of listening to brokenness and of feeling the sadness that shows on the faces of so many people. Lord, don't You think You could just leave me here and give my assignments to someone else?"

As I have reflected on what I wrote, the frightening thing to realize is that God could say Yes. He could leave me alone. In fact, He could let me sit on my small piece of sod throughout all eternity, if I chose to do so. He will allow me the option of ignoring His story and let me concentrate on my own.

But If I do, He will choose someone else to walk with Him in His great adventure of living and loving. He will touch someone else and say, "Come, know the joy of working with Me, and I will show you dreams that you could have never imagined before. It's true that at times you may feel stretched and get breathless and be frightened, but I have equipped and strengthened you for your tasks. I'll not make the footsteps too big for you to follow. Come and climb with Me, and I promise to guide you every step of the way.

"My reward will be a joy and peace that defies all understanding. And my reward will also be other hills to climb, new paths to follow, other responsibilities to carry, and more people to love for My sake. Trust Me. You are able!"

"Be not weary in well doing...The grace of our Lord Jesus Christ be with you all. Amen."